MINT

MW00629622

Pranjal Kamra is a seasoned value investor and a YouTuber with over two million subscribers on his channel. His YouTube channel is the biggest in the financial education domain and aims at empowering investors and disseminating financial awareness. He is the author of an Amazon bestseller, *Investonomy: The Stock Market Guide That Makes You Rich*, and founder and CEO of Finology Ventures Pvt. Ltd.

Pranjal is an alumnus of the National Institute of Securities Market and holds a degree in law from HNLU. His sharp acumen and skills in investing have helped him earn a name for himself at the age of just twenty-seven.

For more information on him and Finology, visit www.finology.in.

MINT YOUR
MONEY

*An Easy Manual to Unlocking
Your Wealth-Creating Potential*

PRANJAL KAMRA

First published by Westland Business, an imprint of Westland Publications Private Limited, in 2021

1st Floor, A Block, East Wing, Plot No. 40, SP Infocity, Dr MGR Salai, Perungudi, Kandanchavadi, Chennai 600096

Westland, the Westland logo, Westland Business and the Westland Business logo are the trademarks of Westland Publications Private Limited, or its affiliates.

ISBN: 9788194879039

Book design by New Media Line Creations, New Delhi 110 062

Printed at Thomson Press (India) Ltd.

Contents

Preface

Let's start with a bitter and stark truth of life—the importance of money. Its value can be understood from the fact that you are reading this! If life for you is just about fulfilling your basic needs, then maybe you have reached the zenith of spirituality. But since you are reading this, it could be assumed that you are an average human being for whom money matters.

You would have surely thought to yourself at some point in life, 'If I had enough money ...' It's funny that nobody knows what 'enough' money actually is; i.e. how much does it amount to? Now, when you are not sure of the amount you wish to have, what happens as a result is that financial planning becomes subjective and is neglected (because planning requires a destination). This is where you need 'personal finance management'. Now, if you're managing your personal finances, and at every step you encounter fine print, 'terms & conditions applied', in other words, you have no clue about the exact financial impact of your actions, you'll be frustrated and eventually drop the idea of managing your finances. But imagine if you could learn simple ways to effectively handle your finances. That would be really helpful, right?

You might think of reaching out to a financial expert for help. The financial industry depends and, in fact, exists on selling you products to help you manage your money. The problem is, most of the financial products being sold to you are not governed by your needs. They are governed by the commission being paid to the agents. In my experience, whoever approaches you, disguised as your well-wisher, pretending to be a part of your family, is exactly the person you should stay away from.

Due to this commission-backed selling, we start living in a mirage, assuming that we have planned well for our kids' education, retirement and medical expenses, and are ready for all contingencies. This is a problem, bigger than the mirage itself. Through this book, I aim to develop independent thinking in you so that you can decide what your needs are and plan accordingly.

Mint Your Money is not just a book, it's a spell of simple financial wisdom for you. Reading this book will help you improve your financial decision-making and take simple small steps in life that can make a huge positive difference later on.

Introduction

The world is full of illusions. What looks right may not be the best choice for you. This is even more true while handling money. There's only one possible outcome when you make a wrong choice with your money—you lose it! So you need to be more cautious in your money matters. If you've got financial goals, the only way to accomplish them is by having the right approach. Now, either you can learn from my experiences, or you can start learning from scratch. You can choose the latter, but that would take time and effort, and you might lose some money as well in the process. The choice is yours.

Think about the ways you spent your money in the past. The problem is that we don't realise the future impact of our actions as we commit them.

We only crib about them once we experience their effect in the future. We should be more cautious in our present actions. But this is easier said than done.

However, those who are cautious with their money (like one of my dear friends, Khushi) experience financial bliss in life. She is sponsoring her son's higher education in a costly university (without taking a loan), taking care of her parents' and in-laws' health expenses, and is able to travel the world without any monetary inhibitions. Before I explain to you as to how she has been able to do this, I would like to tell you a bit about her.

She was born in a middle-class family and faced all those typical financial struggles in life. She was the only child of her parents and eventually became the only breadwinner of the family. She has been working in the private sector for quite some while now, and is currently in a middle-management role. You might be thinking that her current financial status seems unrealistic based on all this. Right?

At this point I want to ask you a simple question:

Who would you consider more successful—Tanya, a person earning ₹60,000 per month, or Khushi, a person earning ₹38,000 per month?

Most of us would say Tanya is more successful.

But that's not the right way of judging success. We have a habit of judging others based on our criteria. So you might say that since Tanya is earning more, she is definitely more successful.

Before proceeding, let me tell you that Tanya is another friend of mine. She and Khushi are from similar backgrounds and have had similar experiences in life but a few small decisions made a huge difference to their lives.

As I told you, Khushi has all expenditures well taken care of, be it her kids' education, marriage, all medical expenses, etc., besides having enough savings for anything unexpected. Tanya, meanwhile, is still paying hefty EMIs and dreads an emergency that would probably drain all her savings! Do you still think that Tanya is more successful?

In my view, success is not about flaunting premium brands or spending lavishly on luxury items. It's about having enough money when you need it the most. I've learnt this from the lives of Khushi and Tanya. Their life stories will open your eyes too.

Cash Flow:
The Incomplete Truth of
Personal Finance

1

Everyone dreams of getting rich and almost all of us try finding ways to do so. Most of us think that having a higher income will make us rich, so if your business earns more profits, or if you get a salary hike, you will be richer. And why wouldn't we think this way? After all, we always associate 'wealth' with our 'income'. But is this the correct approach? Let's talk about the richest man on earth and his 'income'.

Since 2018, Jeff Bezos has been recognised as the world's richest person. Do you think it is because his company makes the most profit or because he draws the highest salary? For the record, in 2018, he drew an annual salary of $80,840 and Amazon (his company) made a profit of $3,033 billion (source: Global 500 by Fortune). It should be noted that

Amazon was not even in the Top 50 most profitable companies of the world in 2018 and Bezos held around only 17% shares of the company.

He is the wealthiest person not because of his monthly income or business profits but because of the valuation of his business holdings, or the assets held by him. We are always so caught up in improvising our income and expenditure account (the one which shows our income and expenses) that we hardly have time to focus on our balance sheet (the one which shows assets and liabilities).

The first time Tanya saved money was to buy a brand-new Hero bicycle. Afterwards, she saved for sunglasses, a badminton racquet, make-up, and so on. She aimed to save more, to spend more. When she started getting a salary, this habit didn't change. She continued to save only to spend on all kinds of luxuries. I cannot name a brand she didn't own. Everybody was mesmerised with her choice of clothing, perfume and shoes. She used to say, 'Never compromise on your shoes; it's the first thing people notice.' She was like an eye-catching flowering plant in the middle of a garden. Always the centre of attraction. She lived a life that was the dream of many. She saved efficiently and spent relentlessly. Her life basically revolved around her income-expenditure statement.

The two wings of your income and expenditure account is nothing but your 'income' and 'expenses'. Your income is money that you receive in exchange for any service, goods, capital, and such. So, your income can be your salary, business profits, interest received on your bank accounts, rents received, and so on. 'Expenses' are nothing but the money spent on your needs, wants and desires. This is how your income and expenditure account will look:

Income & Expenditure Account			
Expenditure	**Amount**	**Income**	**Amount**
'What you spend'		**'What you get'**	
House rent	✓	Salary	✓
Food	✓	Interest	✓
Travel	✓	Bonus	✓
Kids' education	✓	Gifts	✓
Luxuries	✓	Business Profits	✓
Movies	✓		
Transportation	✓		
'Savings'	✓		
(excess of income over expenditures)	XXX		XXX

Now, just to clarify, your outflows can be in the form of contribution to your Provident Fund (PF), money set aside in fixed deposits, etc., but they do not count as expenditures; they are your investments and are classified as 'assets'. Similarly, if you take a loan, it is a cash inflow, but it doesn't count as your income—it's a 'liability'.

A large segment of India's population is quite efficient in saving money. We are born with a frugal mindset. We bargain, we procrastinate expenditures and we save. But the problem is, we never think of anything beyond the income and expenditure account. We want to save money, but why are we saving it? To spend more money in the future. This is a vicious circle of income and expenses. Now, let's talk about assets and liabilities.

A balance sheet records your assets and liabilities. It shows your financial position at any point of time. We consider assets as anything that has a more than reasonable chance of generating a cash inflow in the future. Thus, cash outflow for contributing to PF, buying gold or buying a home are not your expenses but your assets. Liabilities are things that demand a future cash outflow. Your credit card bill and debt are your liabilities. The difference between your assets and liabilities gives your net worth, something that determines your financial strength.

Unlike Tanya, Khushi was not focusing on her income and expenses. She was very frugal-minded, but a happy person. I remember, when Khushi

Personal Balance Sheet			
Liabilities	**Amount**	**Assets**	**Amount**
Credit Card Due	✓	Home	✓
Education Loan	✓	Car	✓
Home Loan	✓	Phone	✓
Personal Loan	✓	Provident Fund	✓
		Mutual Funds	✓
Net-Worth	✓	Investments	✓
(Assets - Liabilities)		Bank	✓
		Cash in hand	✓
	XXX		XXX

got her first salary in 2011, the first thing she did was buy a 5-gram gold coin for approximately ₹13,000 (this grew to ₹25,000 by 2020, when she sold it and bought equity shares for ₹10,000 and furnished her house with the remaining ₹15,000). I hate to break the suspense, but her investment of ₹10,000 in the stock market grew to ₹18,000 in another couple of years. She had bigger and better plans that none of us understood then. She was like a growing tree located in the corner of the garden. Nobody saw it growing, but she managed to grow the roots strong enough to survive every financial turbulence in her life.

Let's get back to 'net worth' (i.e. assets minus liabilities). We often use it as a parameter to gauge a company or any business's financial position. When you buy a car, you record it as an asset, as it can generate a cash inflow at the time of resale. Now tell me, suppose you have a car worth ₹10 lakhs, how much money can you make from it? Even if it is two days old, I am sure that you won't be able to sell it for more than ₹8 lakhs.

In fact, even if you have ₹10 lakhs in your savings bank account, it will lose its value over time. Wondering how?

Let me introduce you to inflation, a phenomenon responsible for the increase in the price of goods and services. It is not a secret that prices of commodities rise automatically with time. Something which was available for ₹100 in 2012 would have cost more than ₹150 in 2015. On an average, the inflation rate in India has been between 4% and 7%. This means your purchasing power decreases 4% to 7% every year. If you are able to buy 100 chocolates for ₹100 today, then due to inflation, you will be able to buy only 96 chocolates for the same amount, the next year.

So, for instance, if prices of commodities rise by 5% every year, while your money rises by 4%, your money is losing its value at a rate of 1% every year. Suppose the cost of college education today is ₹8 lakhs, and it grows by 5% every year, by the time your kid is sixteen, the cost of education will be over ₹17 lakhs. Suppose you already have ₹8 lakhs today, and you decide to keep it aside in a savings bank account providing post-tax returns of 3%, your post-tax corpus (total amount accumulated) will be around ₹12.84 lakhs. That means, even if you have the complete corpus to meet your child's education today, inflation could prevent you from doing so when it's required. In such circumstances, you will need to plan your finances in a way such that you are financially ready to meet all the milestones ahead of you.

Tell me this, who would you consider the wealthiest? Ms A, a person who owns cars worth ₹10 crores, Ms B, a person who has ₹10 crores as cash (with no intention of investing it), Ms C, who has ₹10 crores lying in a savings bank account or Ms D, who has ₹5 crores in a savings bank account and ₹5 crores invested in land?

If you try to decide by accounting net worth, everyone's net worth will be the same in the first year. In just one year, cars will start depreciating by 15% (as per tax laws) and affect Ms A's net worth; Ms B's net worth will remain constant 'in the books' at ₹10 crores; Ms C's net worth will show an increase of approximately 3% (₹30 lakhs) every year; Ms D's accounting net worth will increase by almost ₹15 lakhs (3% of ₹5 crores, as land will be recorded at purchase price only).

In reality, Ms A's worth is less than what is presented in the books because the value of cars will depreciate with a rate of approximately 50% (and sometimes even more depending on the model and manufacturer of the car). Although Ms B's worth appears to be constant, her money is losing value on account of inflation. Ms C seems to be the wealthiest after three years but has still lost money's value to inflation; but sadly, this is not visible in her account. The truth is, it is only Ms D's land which has successfully outperformed inflation and helped Ms D to enhance her existing wealth. Hence, I feel net worth is not an apt parameter when it comes to 'Personal Finance' and you cannot rely on it to meet your financial goals.

Till now, we have discovered an important feature of personal finances: our main motivation can't be to boost income or net worth. So what is that one metric that every individual should focus on?

Personal Capital—that's what you should focus on. It is a concept almost the same as net worth, except that it considers 'True Assets' instead of 'Assets'. True Assets are those assets which are capable of beating inflation in the long run. This implies that, for any

Personal Capital ⊜ True Assets ⊖ Liabilities

asset to be classified as a True Asset and form a part of Personal Capital, it should provide returns at least equal to the rate of inflation.

Your Personal Capital is nothing but that amount of wealth which is working for you. By building your Personal Capital, you are ensuring that your money works for you. Since it is made up of True Assets, which do not lose value to inflation, they are going to be with you during all ups and downs. People say that even your own shadow leaves you at the time of darkness—trust me, your Personal Capital will stand by your side in every situation. Be it a happy occasion like your kid's graduation, or a medical emergency, your Personal Capital is going to be by your side.

Managing your personal finances doesn't aim to make you rich, it aims to protect your existing assets and mobilise them in such a way so as to make you financially independent and pave your way for financial freedom. It's not important to sit on a pile of money, it is just one of those worldly pleasures. It is important to have sufficient money as and when you need it. The goal is to meet all your financial needs and desires at all times.

To achieve this, you need to take care of the five drivers of Personal Capital.

1. *Savings*
2. *Debt*
3. *Investment*
4. *Taxes*
5. *Insurance*

The better you manage these five components, the more handsome your Personal Capital will be.

Module:
Wealth Creation

Savings: The Ignored 'Financial Angel'

2

aving is the first step towards 'Minting Your Money'. Saving money can be compared with charity. Everyone knows and agrees that doing charity is good, but only a few actually do it. All of us say that we should save money, but when we are asked 'How much do you save?', we give reasons like 'Mehangai kafi badh gayi hai (inflation has increased a lot)', 'I encounter newer spends each month', 'One should live in the present and not think much about the future much' or 'I don't earn too much', and so on.

The question is, how can we save money? I remember when I was in college, I used to get ₹5,000 per month as pocket money. I would mostly spend it in the canteen and on books and video games. However, I always thought that if I received ₹8,000 instead, my life would be much more comfortable. When I started my post-graduation, I would get ₹10,000 per month, but again, it was never enough. Having more money never solved my money problems. That is when it hit me—maybe it was not about the amount I was getting but about the way I was spending! It got me thinking.

Now, I'm not the only one who went through a money problem. Everyone has a similar experience, but we don't realise it. Let's understand this mathematically:

Savings = Income – Expenditure

This means that your savings are dependent on not just your income but your expenditure too. At any point of time, you can give a boost to your savings by planning your expenditure well and, conversely, you may have no effect on your savings even after an increase in monthly income if expenditure also increases.

This is what happened with Tanya. She used to board a metro to work, which cost her ₹30 per day. But after getting a raise, she bought a car and drove to work which cost her at least ₹100 per day. This is what we all do, too. Right? As we make more money, we tend to increase our expenditure by spending on some luxuries. This also explains why whatever money we earn is never enough.

Well, it is a recognised fact that millionaires accumulate wealth not just by earning vast amounts but by not spending the money they earn—and instead investing it.

One of the world's greatest investors, Warren Buffett, once said, 'Do not save what is left after spending, but spend what is left after saving.' You must save a portion of your income first and then plan your expenses from the remaining money. I believe that saving is like a healthy meal which should be consumed regularly to have a financially healthy life.

TRANSFORM YOUR
SAVINGS INTO PERSONAL CAPITAL

People often misunderstand their savings as Personal Capital. Savings is that part of your monthly income that you chose not to spend. You might be saving it to spend it in the next sale season, or you might spend it on a vacation, but for now you're saving it. If you channelize your savings correctly, only then can they be treated as the first step towards building your Personal Capital. If you are stuck in the cycle of saving money to spend more, you will never be able to convert it into your Personal Capital.

Savings increase with an increase in income (or decrease in expenditure). Let's take a simple example. If your monthly income (say salary) increases by ₹5,000 and if your expenditure remains constant, then your monthly savings will increase by ₹5,000. But do you know, if you focus your energy on building your Personal Capital, your savings will be capable of enhancing your income? This means that with an increase in savings by ₹5,000, you can get a boost in your monthly income as well. This happens when you gradually enter a loop of wealth creation.

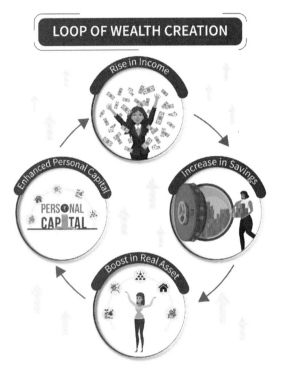

Once you become a part of this loop, you will find yourself creating immense wealth. This life-changing process starts with saving more. When the savings are channelized correctly, your True Assets increase (or your liability reduces by clearing debt). This has a positive effect on your Personal Capital, which in turn increases your income (or reduces your interest expenditure). This again boosts savings. All you need to do is start saving more and channelize the savings by investing them in True Assets.

Suppose you are able to save ₹1 lakh. Invest this in a fixed deposit in a bank. After one year, your income will rise by at least ₹5,000 (depending on the interest rate and your income tax bracket), resulting in an increase in your savings (from ₹1 lakh to ₹1,05,000), and when you reinvest this, you enter the loop of wealth creation.

This loop is fuelled by your savings, and I cannot stress enough on its importance in our lives. Savings gain even more importance once you decide to focus on your Personal Capital.

Suppose you have just ₹1,000 in your bank account. Even if you invest it in an instrument providing 200% returns (although it's highly unlikely you'll find anything like this), you will be able to make only ₹2,000 for yourself. On the other hand, if you save ₹1 lakh and the return on investment is a nominal 10%, even then you will make ₹10,000. So the initial corpus is important and it can be boosted through savings and savings only.

Here's a prelude to get you excited—do you know that by saving just ₹100 per day, you may be able to become a crorepati in thirty years? Don't start calculating right away; I'll tell you how. As of now, do you still underestimate the power of savings?

Budgeting: As Simple as It Can Be

3

I met Khushi at her thirty-fifth birthday party. There was not a single change in her lifestyle. Still guided by her philosophy of 'saada jeevan ucch vichar'. I couldn't resist, so I asked her, how did she manage to do it all? As far as I remember, she never spent lavishly, but that never meant she wasn't spending anything at all. She lived a comfortable life, fulfilled all her dreams and travelled a lot. She had just one answer for it—budgeting.

She created a budget using the famous 50-30-20 rule. The rule says that you should spend a maximum of 50% of your monthly earnings for essentials like food and shelter, not more than 30% of your earnings on wants and luxuries like fancy dinners, EMIs and such, and save at least 20% for your future.

Following this rule diligently in your monthly budgeting will introduce some financial discipline in your life. You would've noticed, the rule doesn't stop you from spending on luxuries. It just puts a limit to the expenses. This will help you to avoid overspending and save more.

Can the 50-30-20 rule be tweaked based upon your financial condition? Yes. Here's how: If you have not planned earlier and your debt has piled up, then you can create a debt repayment focused plan with, say, a 35-45-20 break-up. In this situation, you can use 35% for essential expenses, another 45% of your earnings for debt settlement, and the remaining 20% for savings. This will ensure that most of your money is rightly channelized to take care of your financial past (debt), present (monthly expenditure), and future (savings).

Also, if you want to accelerate the process of wealth creation, you can create an aggressive wealth creation budget with a 40-40-20 percentage break-up. In this, you can put 40% of your earnings in investments, keep another 40% for essential expenses, and the remaining 20% for everything else.

Khushi started with a salary of ₹38,000 per month. She had very few responsibilities at that time and was thus able to save a substantial portion of the salary. As soon as she received money in her bank account, the first thing she did was to set aside 20% money for her future. This money was utilised to buy only True Assets.

Please note that you need to save at least 20% of your income, come what may. If you are not able to save at least 20% of your monthly income, then you need to budget properly.

Many people are simply afraid of the term 'budgeting'. But budgeting is not as complicated as it sounds. You don't have to start preparing balance sheets for yourself and indulge in financial modelling. Budgeting is nothing but managing your expenses, that is, allocating portions of your income for individual purposes or essentials and not spending more than the specified limits. Giving labels to your money will help you control your cravings and prevent thoughtless spending.

Many people believe that they do not need to plan their spending because of a host of reasons. They think that they earn enough to pay their bills, they are debt-free, and are still left with some money which can be put into savings or can be invested. But they do not understand that budgeting can help maximise their savings and investments. It can help identify the additional or unnecessary expenses which can be cut down, and the money can be put to better use.

Budgeting is not about restricting yourself. Rather, it aims at giving you the financial freedom to achieve your goals. It is not about feeling bad or guilty about your spending habits. It just records the expenses and gives you an idea of whether you are spending more than you should. It is an excellent tool that can help you strengthen your financial stability at the core. Budgeting helps you plan your spending and thus has a direct impact on your expenses, debt level, savings and investments. It's all about effectively using your hard-earned money or putting every rupee you earn to work. This remarkable tool helps in developing a habit of systematic financial planning. Overall, it lets you know about your financial situation so that you can live within your means. It also reduces financial stress by tracking your expenses and giving you control over your money.

KNOW YOUR BUDGET

You cannot manage your expenses if you are not aware of them. Similarly, you cannot budget properly if you don't know what your budget is made up of. The two major constituents of your budget are static budget and flexible budget.

A static budget consists of values that are fixed and do not change throughout the budget period. Examples are your monthly rent, loan premium and any investment premium. A flexible budget includes items that are not constant, such as expenses on clothing, travel and outings, festival expenses and other personal expenses. Such expenses are made under your discretion and you have the power to control your them.

Budgeting is simply a spending plan that balances your expenses with income. The static part of a budget makes you aware of your fixed payments, and after considering the flexible costs, you can forecast your expenses. You can easily identify the months of high and low expenses and prepare a financial plan accordingly to achieve goals. You can save money for a vacation, a new vehicle, a new home or renovations, a retirement fund, any other investments, or an emergency fund.

Although the best way to manage finances is unique for every person, following are some key points to remember to succeed in budget planning:

- Keep your static budget as low as possible.
- Spend less than you earn.
- Create a budget periodically (preferably monthly).
- Track the actual cash flows against the planned budget.
- Make changes in your next budget as necessary.

HOW TO CREATE A BUDGET?

Before proceeding to create a budget, you should have an objective in mind. It can be settling a debt, saving for something specific, and so on. This goal-setting is not a one-time process but rather an evolving one. You can change money allocation as your budget objective changes. However, it is highly recommended that the sequence of your goals be maintained as follows:

1. Create an emergency fund.
2. Settle your debt.
3. Create or enhance Personal Capital.

You can create your own budget based on your financial goals. Your budget would be a private affair, as you would be the best person to know your income and judge your expenditure. But there's a common checklist that you can follow. Here's what you need to remember:

- Involve all stakeholders who are a part of your budget (it may be your spouse, parents, etc.).
- Create a list of all your income or cash inflows (from employer, side business, passive income, etc.).
- List all the expenses or cash outflows (static and flexible expenses).
- Allocate suitable money to each of your essential expenses.
- Settle your liabilities first and pay whoever you owe as the first step of cash outflow.
- Stop using credit cards.
- Start allocating money for an emergency fund.

- Set goals with time horizons and allocate some portion of earnings toward them.
- Always remember to allocate at least 20% of your earnings for savings and investments.
- Check whether you are spending less than your earnings.
- Track your spending regularly (make it a habit).
- Check what costs you can cut down and what you can do to increase your income or cash inflows.
- Reward yourself for achieving a goal in your budget to motivate yourself for the next target.
- If you are finding it difficult to manage, then try to find answers to these three questions:

  1. *Are you practical about your goals?*
  2. *Are you too restrictive?*
  3. *Are you able to reduce unnecessary expenses?*

A Fund in Need
Is a Fund Indeed

4

A colleague once suggested to Tanya that they should, together, start investing in stocks or Mutual Funds to generate a pool for retirement. Tanya knew that risks and rewards go hand in hand and that no investment option is devoid of risks. So she refused to invest as she could not afford to lose her 'savings'.

A few months later, another friend of Tanya's suggested a small business opportunity, capable of good growth over time. Tanya again turned it down as she couldn't take any risks.

A couple of years later, the pandemic (Covid-19) forced a crisis and, due to the lockdown, everyone had to stay wherever they were. All economic activities were at a standstill. Tanya was also required to stay safe at home and not come to the office. She was asked to take leave without pay.

In a situation like this, paying off EMIs and monthly expenditures can become a burden. The fear of a deadly virus outside, and the fear of losing all the savings inside—forget about Personal Capital. Tanya's mental and physical health crumbled.

Surprises and mishaps do not ask for permission to enter your life. Change is permanent. Nobody has control over events and there can be many such unprecedented events. They might include a job lay-off, emergency health expenditure, monetary losses, family crises or a pandemic—you cannot avoid them. All you can do is stay prepared. Stay prepared for any financial shock with your own shock absorber. This shock absorber is called an emergency fund.

This is the first action in financial planning that ensures your basic lifestyle remains unaffected, and you don't have to seek additional debt or a loan at the time of crises. This will not only have your back during calamities but also enable you to fly high by taking calculated risks through suitable investments.

HOW MUCH OF AN EMERGENCY FUND DO YOU NEED?

Every individual has a unique lifestyle because of several factors. They have different income levels, needs and wants, have a different number of dependents, and so on. Hence, the size of an emergency fund will be different for every person. I strongly recommend that you have funds available at any time to meet your monthly expenses for at least six months. These should include costs related to all the essentials or for all the basic survival needs and any fixed obligations like EMIs, school fees and such. Thus, ideally, your emergency fund should consist of your six months' expenditure.

WHERE SHOULD YOU
PARK YOUR EMERGENCY FUND?

An emergency fund is the most crucial part of managing your personal finances. It provides you with a strong base to start building your Personal Capital. Without an emergency fund, I would advice against investing your money anywhere or spending on luxuries. Irrespective of your age, gender or current income, the first application of your money should be to build a strong emergency fund and use it only at the time of emergencies. Think of it as dry fruits or preserved food—they may not be a necessity for life but, if you've got nothing to eat, they will become crucial.

Now, your emergency fund should be parked such that it is easily accessible (liquid) and does not lose its value over time. The problem with parking money anywhere is that it comes with risk. If you store your emergency fund in the form of cash, it loses its value over time due to inflation and there is the risk of theft. So, where should you park your money? How can you make your emergency fund a part of your True Assets? Here are a few options available to you.

Savings Bank Account

A savings bank account provides a nominal interest rate (3% approximately) payable every quarter. You have to pay income tax on this interest earned (it enjoys a certain level of tax exemption though). This return does not beat inflation and hence it cannot be classified as your True Assets. Some banks may offer a slightly higher interest rate, but they might add a condition of a higher minimum balance. There is minimal risk involved because a problem can happen only in case of bank failure, that is, if the bank goes out of business.

Bank deposits have an insurance cover of ₹5 lakhs as per the terms of the Deposit Insurance and Credit Guarantee Corporation (DICGC), a subsidiary of the Reserve Bank of India (RBI). These cover all types of bank deposits under an individual's name. If you have deposits of less than ₹5 lakhs, then you will get your money back in case of a bank failure. But if you have more than ₹5 lakhs, then you will lose money. So in terms of safety, ₹5 lakhs is risk-free in a savings bank account. At the same time, it provides utmost liquidity. However, the return doesn't beat inflation, and hence, your money will lose value over time.

Term Deposits

A term deposit is a financial instrument that allows you to deposit money for a fixed period in exchange for a higher return. This fixed period may vary from a few weeks to a few years. Term deposits are also referred to as Certificate of Deposits (CDs). These instruments provide the same level of security as in the case of a savings account. The higher returns come at a price: the fixed duration, and you may have to incur penalties in case of premature withdrawals. Their liquidity is less than that of a savings bank account, and thus, it may not be liquid enough to be your emergency fund.

The two major types of term deposits are fixed deposit (FD) and recurring deposit (RD). Fixed deposits are the type of term deposits wherein you have to deposit a lump-sum amount at the beginning, for a fixed duration. This duration may vary from a period of seven days to ten years. The return or the interest earned depends on the tenure of the deposit. The interest rate may vary from 3.3% to 8%. Senior citizens get higher returns, which may be 0.25% to 0.75% higher than regular FDs. Recurring deposits are the types of term deposits where you have the flexibility to deposit in instalments for a fixed duration. This can help you build financial discipline and save a fixed amount every month.

A term deposit can be classified as a True Asset if the interest earned from it is capable of beating inflation in the long run, but the problem is they do not provide sufficient liquidity to the depositor. And, this is a big problem because the very objective of an emergency fund is to provide liquidity at the time of need. So, even after delivering inflation-beating returns, term deposits can only be an alternative destination to park your emergency fund. You may have better options available based on liquidity. Besides this, a major disadvantage associated with term deposits is that you'll have to discontinue it in full whenever you are in need. What this means is, you cannot withdraw in parts. So, even if you need only 5% of your term deposit amount, you'll have to withdraw 100% of it.

Sweep-In Account

A sweep-in account is an advanced feature of savings bank accounts. It is like a savings-cum-fixed-deposit account with the features of both, so you get higher returns and higher liquidity—the best place to store your emergency fund indeed. In such accounts, the funds exceeding a certain level are automatically transferred into a higher interest-earning term deposit at the end of each business day. Whenever your balance in the account exceeds the threshold limit, then the surplus amount automatically gets transferred to the FD account that generates higher returns. This feature of the transfer of surplus money to the FD account is called a sweep-in facility. There are no restrictions on the amount you can withdraw, so you can use all of it, including the swept-in money lying in fixed deposit, whenever required. You can get your normal savings bank account converted into a sweep-in account at no extra cost.

In fact, I would strongly advise that you convert your current account (which does not earn any interest) into a sweep-in account. This will enable you to earn interest on the excess balance lying in your regular business account.

Sweep-Out Account

Another option is a sweep-out account, where you not only earn the same interest from your regular term deposit but are also allowed to issue cheques from it. This provides you with a higher liquidity than a regular term-deposit account. Even if you need to withdraw a partial amount, the rest of the balance continues to earn interest in a regular manner, therefore eliminating a major disadvantage associated with term deposits.

You can park your money in any of the options we have discussed above or in any other manner, but always consider the following things:

- Is your money safe and secure from market fluctuations?
- Is it easy to access when needed?
- What is the interest earned?
- What are the conditions of deposits and withdrawal?

If you park your money in a term deposit (that pays higher interest), sweep-in account or a sweep-out account, you will be able to protect your emergency fund from inflation and it is more likely to be counted as your True Asset.

I've observed people parking their emergency fund in equity schemes, liquid Mutual Funds and such, which are not immune from market fluctuations. This may result in the fund losing its value and, more importantly, giving you a financial shock during an emergency. They can be a good investment option, but not the right place for your emergency fund.

Smart Ways to Save More

5

With savings, emergency funds and proper budgeting, you can live a financially healthy life. But we can always save some more by slightly improving our lifestyle or by slightly changing our habits.

STOP USING CREDIT CARDS

If you are using credit cards, you might end up making impulse purchases. According to a study on the psychology of spending, pain centres get activated when you buy with cash, but there is no such activation when you buy with a credit card. The willingness to pay increases with a credit card. So, if you pay for things with plastic, you tend to spend more than when you pay with cash.

KEEP YOUR EMERGENCY FUND
IN A SEPARATE BANK ACCOUNT

Keep your emergency funds in a separate bank account (preferably a sweep-in or sweep-out account) and don't opt for a debit card or net banking. This will ensure that you don't lose money to impulsive purchases, mistakes or oversight (you will not be able to spend that money on unnecessary things or while shopping). However, at the time of emergencies, you can easily write yourself a cheque.

SELL UNNECESSARY ITEMS

This will bring in some money, save space and allow you to analyse your past spending habits. Don't think of it as a harmful activity; instead, enjoy the process.

CANCEL YOUR UNNECESSARY SUBSCRIPTIONS

It is an excellent option to subscribe to services that you utilise regularly and thus save money. But with your changing lifestyle and needs, you must be mindful about your subscriptions. Keep looking for cheaper alternatives. Perhaps you do not require a particular service anymore. These subscriptions may be your gym membership, magazine subscriptions, video streaming services and mobile apps with monthly fees, among others.

AVOID IMPULSE PURCHASES

The primary reason behind extra spending is impulse purchases, and most of the time you end up buying unnecessary items just because of your mood, or impressive marketing. Therefore, give yourself time and think a bit before making a purchase, and try to stick to your shopping list.

START A PIGGY BANK

Every paisa counts when it comes to saving. Try out this old-world practice. Gather all the loose change lying around in your house and put it in a piggy bank. Create a habit of putting small amounts in the piggy bank. This will not create huge wealth but will help you and your kids develop a habit of saving.

USE THE ENVELOPE METHOD FOR BUDGETING

This is a traditional way of planning your budget, and it could also help you save cleverly. In this method, I suggest that you withdraw your salary at the beginning of the month. After identifying your static and flexible needs, you can divide your earned money and put it in envelopes for designated purposes. The amount set aside for static expenses will remain as it is, but the same for flexible expenses can be under-utilised or occasionally may be over-utilised.

The objective here is, you should try to not over-utilise what is in your envelopes, which helps in controlling spending habits. In fact, if any amount is under-utilised, then you can transfer that money for savings or investment purposes or for settling your debts. Since you will be spending in cash, you will feel a pinch every time you over-utilise what is in an envelope or overspend. This will induce self-discipline with regards to your spending.

The one disadvantage to this method is that, withdrawing cash at the beginning of the month means you will not earn the interest that you would have if it had remained in a savings account. You wouldn't want to lose out on the interest, and therefore, you can rectify this by having a separate bank account where you could set aside your savings in the beginning of the month itself. But remember, get back to the bank account (and stop withdrawing cash) only after you've attained self-discipline.

USE APPS

There are a variety of apps available that track all your monthly expenses where you can plan your budget as per your desired goals. This can be an easy and efficient way to plan your finances because the app tracks all your expenses and categorises them with minute details (that it gets from your text messages of any amount being debited or credited to your account).

Building your Personal Capital is all about your choices. There are going to be sacrifices and you might have to make decisions that you may not like, such as cutting back on reckless spending, but at the end of the day, it is going to be worth it.

You have to remember that even if you have the latest smartphone, someone somewhere definitely owns a better phone; if you wear a Rolex, someone somewhere shows off a more expensive watch. These comparisons have no end. These things can just provide you with a momentary illusion of satisfaction but are not good for your Personal Capital. However, as they say, 'You can take a horse to the water but you can't make it drink.' Similarly, whatever information I may provide, it is finally your decision to save and enhance your Personal Capital, or keep spending on and on...

Module:
Debt

Introduction to Debt 6

While interacting with your elders, you would have realised that there's a dreadful financial ghost which can eat away all your savings. It possesses the power to financially destabilise you and even make you beg! This ghost is debt. Yes, that's how debt is referred to traditionally in families. Whenever you may have discussed taking a loan for your car or house or education, your elders would have surely guided you to first think carefully about how you will pay it back. In fact, they might have asked you to avoid it, to the extent possible. Isn't that right?

Let's look at the other side of the picture. Can you name one successful industrialist or businessperson in the world who never took a loan? If debt was such a ghost, as we have been told, how did it help these business people become big tycoons? That's confusing! Is debt a boon or an evil? You will be able to decide for yourself by the end of this section.

Meanwhile, let's get back to Tanya and Khushi, and see how debt affected their lives. It so happened that both of them wanted to take their careers to the next level. So, they decided to pursue a distance MBA programme to enhance their skills. The offer was great. They could go to work normally and just had to spend three to four hours every week for this MBA programme. At the end, new doors with better job prospects would open for them. But there was one problem. For the purpose of admission to the B-School, they were required to pay the fees of ₹5 lakhs in advance, as a lump sum. Both of them understood that the only way was to borrow money. So both of them took an education loan of ₹5 lakhs, at the same interest rate (of 12% per annum compounded monthly). But they chose different repayment terms.

Tanya wanted to keep her monthly repayment amounts as small as possible so that she didn't feel the pinch on her monthly budget. She opted for a plan with equated monthly instalments (EMIs) of ₹7,000 for 10.5 years. 'Only ₹7,000 every month! That's quite affordable,' she thought.

On the other hand, Khushi was quite sceptical about taking a loan. She knew that this was important but she wanted to get rid of her debt as soon as possible. So, based on her monthly savings (that were close to ₹25,000 per month), she chose a plan with an EMI of ₹20,000 per month for around 2.5 years.

Who, according to you, made the right decision? What would you do? Save your thoughts for later. Once you finish reading this segment, have a look again at your answers.

The Toxic Relationship Between Debt and Personal Capital

7

I have observed that people usually give priority to conserving cash outflows rather than focusing on their Personal Capital. They tend to make choices which appear to be easy on their pockets. For example, if you are given an option between LED bulbs with the same power but priced at ₹100 and ₹1,000, which one are you most likely to choose? The cheaper one, of course! Even though it may be possible that the one costing ₹1,000 will serve you at least three years, while the one costing ₹100 would last for hardly two months. Similarly, it is not necessary that every cash outflow adversely affects your Personal Capital, just like a cash outflow involving repayment of debt saves you interest cost.

Tanya chose the option with a lower cash outflow of ₹7,000 per month, but its impact on her Personal

Capital is very large. Let us see how debt impacts your Personal Capital.

In the beginning, I mentioned the formula

Personal Capital = True Assets – Liabilities

Liabilities refer to anything that would cause a cash outflow. Now, whenever you take a loan, there will be the following impact on your Personal Capital:

1. At the time of taking a loan, the increase in liability would reduce your Personal Capital. This loan amount is that part of your capital which is not working for you. Instead, it makes you work as you have to pay an interest on it.

2. As you pay off the loan, your liabilities start decreasing but so do your deposits. This reduces your True Assets as well, because the instalments are paid off from your monthly savings (which would otherwise have been a part of your Personal Capital).

3. The interest paid on a loan is again a reduction from your True Assets as it will be paid from your savings, thereby negatively impacting your Personal Capital. Once this interest starts compounding—that is, you start paying interest on interest—your Personal Capital starts decreasing rapidly.

THE EFFECTS OF COMPOUNDING

Compounding results in exponential multiplication, and hence it has the power to create immense wealth for you, or pile up your debt to an extent that you may never be able to pay it off! When the money starts working for you, it can increase your Personal Capital by manifolds. But, in case of debts, the interest just keeps adding to your amount outstanding and eats up your Capital.

If you noticed, the interest rate on the loan was 12% compounded monthly. When I say 12%, most of us will calculate interest as ₹12,000 per year on ₹1 lakh. But, read it carefully, it says 12% compounded monthly; this means, the effective annual interest rate on the loan is around 12.68%. When the interest is 'compounded monthly', the interest on the second month is not calculated on the actual money borrowed but on the money borrowed and interest of the first month combined.

For example, if I borrow ₹5 lakhs at 12% per annum (simple interest), the interest charged will be ₹60,000 per year or ₹5,000 per month. However, if I borrow the amount at an interest rate of 12% compounded monthly, the interest of the first month is computed as 1% of the amount outstanding, which is ₹5,000. This raises the amount outstanding to ₹5,05,000, and hence the interest charged in the second month is ₹5,050 (1% of ₹5,05,000), and so on.

MONTH	INTEREST	AMOUNT OUTSTANDING
1	5,000.00	5,05,000.00
2	5,050.00	5,10,050.00
3	5,100.50	5,15,150.50
4	5,151.51	5,20,302.01
5	5,203.02	5,25,505.03
6	5,255.05	5,30,760.08

The sum of ₹5 lakhs borrowed at merely 1% per month has grown to ₹5,30,760 in just six months, the amount of interest being ₹30,760. If the money was borrowed at a simple interest rate of 12%, then the amount of interest would be 30,000. The difference of ₹760 is made by compounding.

Banks deliberately quote interest rates in such a way that the customers tend to believe they are paying a lower interest rate (although it's not true). When Khushi and Tanya took their loans with an effective interest rate of 12.78% per annum, they were tricked into believing that interest rates were just 1% per month.

Now, the effect of compounding is fuelled by the duration of the loan. While paying an EMI of ₹7,000 for a loan of ₹5 lakhs, Tanya had to pay an interest of approximately ₹3,82,000 over 10.5 years. This was in addition to the repayment of the principal amount of ₹5 lakhs. The interest amounted to 76% of the total sum borrowed. On the other hand, the interest paid by Khushi roughly amounted to ₹78,000, which was almost one-fifth of Tanya's. This also implies that after complete repayment of the loan of ₹5 lakhs, Tanya's Personal Capital reduced by nearly ₹8,82,000, while Khushi's Personal Capital took a toll of ₹5,78,000.

Let us see what happened when Tanya repaid ₹7,000 every month. What would be the amount of loan outstanding after six months?

MONTH	INTEREST	AMOUNT REPAID	AMOUNT OUTSTANDING
1	5,000.00	7,000.00	4,98,000.00
2	4,980.00	7,000.00	4,95,980.00
3	4,959.80	7,000.00	4,93,939.30
4	4,939.40	7,000.00	4,91,879.20
5	4,918.79	7,000.00	4,89,797.99
6	4,897.98	7,000.00	4,87,695.97

After paying EMIs worth ₹7,000 for six months: Payment made was ₹42,000 and her liability at the end of the sixth month stood at ₹4,87,695.

Compare this with the example where no repayment was done, and the principal at the end of the sixth month stood at ₹5,30,760.

As a result of paying EMIs, the reduction in liability is positively impacted. It should be noted that, after making a repayment of ₹42,000, the loan outstanding after six months reduced by almost ₹43,000 (₹5,30,760 − ₹4,87,695).

With Khushi, since she was paying an EMI of ₹20,000 every month, the amount of loan outstanding after six months was ₹4,07,719. In comparison with Tanya, Khushi paid additional instalments of ₹13,000 per month (a sum of ₹78,000 in excess of Tanya in six months), but the difference between their outstanding loan differs by almost ₹80,000 (₹4,87,695 − ₹4,07,719). This difference is on account of reduced interest expenditure in lieu of bigger instalments. Since Khushi's loan duration was way shorter than Tanya's, she was able to reduce the damage caused by compounding of interest.

Good Loan
vs
Bad Loan

8

Everybody knows that debts or loans generally come with an inherent risk and additional costs to your monthly budget. They can be in the form of a home loan, education loan, credit cards or EMIs; debts are unavoidable in certain circumstances. When it comes to personal finances, it may not be possible to avoid liability altogether. But it is always possible to plan it cautiously.

The first question that should come into your mind before deciding to opt for a loan is whether it is a good loan or a bad loan.

Just as we separate the whites from the dark clothes to preserve the colour while washing, similarly, to deal with your debt better, we will begin by distinguishing between good and bad loans.

Now, everyone knows a loan comes with an additional obligation to your monthly budget, and it is required to be paid back. So how can it be good?

A GOOD LOAN

A good loan is more like an investment made to improve your overall financial position. That means, a loan will be considered as a 'good' loan if it increases your Personal Capital in the long run by either growing in value or by helping you generate income. These are generally low-cost debts which can be repaid in affordable instalments. Some examples of good loans:

Education Loan

An education loan is like investing in oneself. First of all, it will improve your employability and pave your way for a well-paying career, ensuring that you will have a source of income to provide for your needs. Secondly, interest rates are generally very low for such loans and the loans are to be repaid in very affordable instalments after you complete your education. Also, there are certain income tax benefits associated with the repayment of an education loan.

Home Loan

Home loans are again one of the cheapest kinds of loans available in the market. A home loan helps you acquire an asset whose value generally appreciates with time and it will save you rental expenditures, thereby reducing your monthly spending. The repayment is usually spread over a considerable period, like twenty years, and repayment of a home loan also comes with income tax benefits.

Other Loans

A small business loan can also be considered as a 'good' loan if you are confident that it holds financial benefits in the future. The interest charged might be a little high on them, but your business's future profits may ultimately help to boost your Personal Capital in the long run.

While planning your personal finances, if you opt for a good loan, don't forget to evaluate the risks associated with it. For instance, when you take an education loan, the loan doesn't guarantee you a stable and well-paying job. Or, when you take a home loan, there will be additional expenditures like municipal taxes and insurances.

BAD LOANS

Bad loans are the ones that are taken for assets that might not be able to generate future income or taken for those goods whose value depreciates really fast or for items of personal consumption. These loans are available at a very high interest rate. Thus, such loans tend to destroy your wealth. If you are ever stuck with a bad loan, try to pay it off as early as possible. Some examples of bad loans:

Credit Cards

Credit card loans, generally, are not considered as a good loan as they have very high interest rates. They are also accompanied by very high maintenance costs. Apart from the associated costs, very often credit cards encourage non-essential purchases and increase your debt. So if you have a credit card, you need to manage it wisely.

Car Loans

I completely understand that, in the twenty-first century, one car might be an absolute necessity and you can't always rely on cabs or public transport— but taking a loan to buy a second car … really? It is a costly affair to buy one, and as soon as you move it out of the showroom, it loses at least 20% of its value.

And by the time the loan is paid off completely, the cost of the car turns very high while the value it may provide will be way too little.

Let's talk some numbers:

Suppose you buy a car for ₹5 lakhs without taking any loans and you are expecting to use it for five years.

Now, say you run it for 1,00,000 km, the cost of petrol is ₹80 per litre, and the car can run for 20 km per litre of petrol. Let us say that you need a driver too, costing ₹10,000 per month.

Let's list the expenses over five years:

Nature of expenditure	Amount
Cost of car	₹5,00,000
Cost of driver (10,000*12*5)	₹6,00,000
Petrol cost @ ₹4/km (4*1,00,000)	₹4,00,000
Less resale value	(₹1,00,000)
Total cost for owning the car	₹14,00,000

The total cost of owning a car comes to ₹14 lakhs, ignoring servicing costs, other mandatory maintenance costs, interest costs and insurance premiums.

If you just took a cab, it costs a maximum of ₹12 per km, and would cost ₹12 lakhs for five years in the above example. And this facility comes with the additional benefit of not worrying about parking or running out of petrol. Do consider this before buying a second car.

Other Loans

Today, loans can be taken for almost everything— mobile phones, laptops, home appliances, jewellery or even a luxurious holiday. You simply have to repay the money in EMIs. You need to be aware that all these easy loans are just marketing schemes to expand the customer base so that the products are not limited to the super rich. The plans often sound very attractive and pocket-friendly, but the retail stores, as well as the banking partners, tend to make huge money out of these through interest costs, additional charges and processing fees. These types of loans just promote consumption in society.

HOW CAN YOU DECIDE WHETHER A DEBT IS A GOOD LOAN OR A BAD LOAN?

You should always remember that the person selling you a loan doesn't have your best interests at heart. They are trying to pitch it to you just to meet their targets. Once you agree to the debt, you will end up with months of your salary tied up in EMIs. So follow this checklist:

1. Ask yourself if you really need that loan.
2. Check the interest rate—it should not be very high.
3. Revisit the repayment terms—the instalments should be affordable.
4. Review your ability to pay back the loan. Make provisions for contingencies.
5. Try to make the down payment as high as possible. This will reduce the interest cost on the purchase.

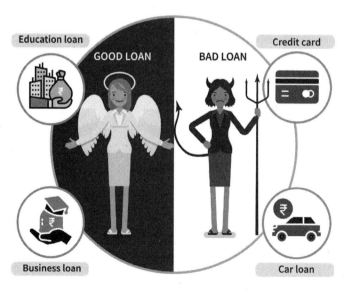

Procuring loans to buy assets like a house or a computer for your work will help you make or save money in the future, and will help you enhance your Personal Capital in the long run. But taking loans to buy a fancy car that you cannot afford or any other consumer goods just adds to your liability by demanding more cash outflows. For example, if you took a loan for a vacation, apart from the loan and interest amount, your Personal Capital will further deteriorate because of the amount you spend on shopping for the trip and on the trip. The interest rates on bad loans are generally high, and by the time you finish repaying the loan, the value of the commodity is often reduced by more than 50%. Thus, invest in buying True Assets, not liabilities. Tanya and Khushi opted for an educational loan—a good choice to make.

HOW DO EMIS WORK?

In India, household debt has been rising at a tremendous rate in the last few decades. One of the primary reasons behind it is the facility of paying via EMIs. EMIs, or Equated Monthly Instalments, have made even expensive products accessible to all. You can buy any product of your choice and pay for it in small monthly instalments. Buying an iPhone for

₹80,000 may seem very expensive, but buying it for ₹1,500 per month seems affordable and practical. A small amount gets deducted from your account every month, and thus you don't feel like a hole has been burnt in your pockets. So EMIs provide a way where you can live beyond your means at the expense of spending your future earnings. As soon as you buy a product on EMI, you are bound to set aside a part of your future earnings for repayment of the debt. It might be uncertain whether you will get that salary, but the application of it is pre-decided.

Nowadays we find that retailers offer 'no-cost' EMIs on almost all products. But are they really 'no cost'? Are retailers so desperate to sell their products that they would give them away at no interest cost? Isn't this like a free lunch? Let us unfold this mystery.

How do retailers actually make money on such offers?

When we talk about no-cost EMI, the interest component of the loan is often camouflaged in the form of processing fees and other charges. Sometimes, while opting for no-cost EMIs, you are actually deprived of certain discounts that would have been available if you had paid the whole amount upfront. These constitute the cost of your debt.

Now, while shopping online, you may see the 'no-cost EMIs available' message next to the product. Such options are made available by the platforms to increase their volumes. So if the discount offered on the product remains the same, irrespective of the payment option you choose, you are actually not paying any additional cost. However, the monthly instalment will still be a part of your fixed monthly obligation, and you will have to budget it accordingly.

In reality, EMIs can act as a chain tying you to an undesirable situation. The interest accrues every month, and you need to repay the instalment. I have many friends who are stuck with a job they don't like, just because they have to keep paying their EMIs. Because of the burden of EMIs, they just cannot afford to lose their jobs. Thus, it becomes vital for you to analyse your existing situation and opt for a loan only if you can really afford it.

It is really cool to have that latest iPhone, but it is even cooler to be debt-free.

Debt Trap

9

Heard of a rat trap? It's a device used to trap rodents. There's a bait, like a piece of cheese, kept in the middle of the trap. The rat or mouse gets attracted by the bait and is not able to resist it. But when it goes to grab the piece of cheese, it gets trapped. The greed of the rodent has put it in the clutches of the trap.

This is the simple principle based on which a debt trap works.

Let's understand this through Tanya's transactions. Suppose, instead of repaying ₹7,000 per month, she paid an instalment of ₹4,000 per month on her loan. Let us see her financial condition after six months:

Month	Interest	Amount Repaid	Amount Outstanding
1	5,000.00	4,000.00	5,01,000.00
2	5,010.00	4,000.00	5,02,010.00
3	5,020.10	4,000.00	5,03,030.10
4	5,030.30	4,000.00	5,04,060.40
5	5,040.60	4,000.00	5,05,101.01
6	5,051.01	4,000.00	5,06,152.02

For the first month, the interest accrued is ₹5,000 while the instalment paid is ₹4,000. The amount of instalment paid every month is not sufficient to cover the interest cost, hence, the amount outstanding keeps on increasing, even after paying regular instalments. If the circumstances do not change, Tanya will never be able to repay her debt. This is known as a debt trap—a situation where it is very difficult for a borrower to pay back their loan.

This is how it happens. An EMI comprises two parts. One part pays interest on the loan and the second part repays the principal amount. A debt trap happens when the instalments are enough to pay only the interest amount (or, worse, a part of it) and fail to repay any of the principal amount of the loan. Thus, the amount of loan outstanding does not decrease even after paying all the instalments on time.

Now, in order to get some relief, the borrower may re-borrow or restructure the payment, but they will just remain in this cycle unless the instalments start paying off the principal component of the loan, besides the accrued interest.

One potential debt trap near you is your credit card. The amount you charge on it is like a loan taken from the issuer of the card. You will be required to pay off all the purchases you made in a billing cycle before a specific due date. If you can clear the entire balance, no interest will be charged to you. That means the loan that you took from the issuer of the credit card was interest-free. However, if you are not able to clear the whole outstanding balance, you can make a part payment and you will be charged interest on the outstanding amount. This interest is generally very high. If this part payment is lower than the minimum payment specified, you will be liable for additional charges. This means, if you fail to clear the bill as well as make the minimum payment, you will not only be charged with interest but a penalty as well. If you make just the minimum payment, you will be charged with interest only.

One mistake that people make, which ends up burning a hole in their pockets, is they pay off just the minimum payment mentioned in their credit card bill. They believe that they'll be able to slowly clear the entire debt. However, they are charged with a hefty interest every month, so the amount of credit outstanding keeps shooting up. Ultimately, if the borrower misses clearing one bill, it becomes harder for them to pay it off.

Here, I would like to remind you that just because you have a credit limit of ₹1 lakh in your credit card, it does not mean that you can afford a credit limit of ₹1 lakh. Don't max out the card every month. Be cautious of your financial health.

USING YOUR CREDIT CARD(S) SMARTLY

One thing worth noting about a credit card is that it is an interest-free loan if you clear the entire bills regularly, before the due dates. You can take advantage of this by earning interest on your savings bank account while paying through your credit cards, and once your credit card bill is generated, you can pay it off well within time to avoid any interest.

Let's see how it works.

Suppose I have ₹1 lakh in my savings bank account, earning an interest of 5% per annum (via the sweep-in feature). I used my credit card to pay my bills of ₹1 lakh on 2 January. On 1 February, my credit card bill will be generated, and I will be given ten days to clear my dues. Let's say I clear my dues using the balance in my savings bank account on 9 February. Thus I will earn an interest of at least Rs 500 on the balance that was lying in my savings account for this time period.

This is how credit cards can work to your advantage. You just have to be careful about clearing dues on time and not spending more than you can actually afford. Most of all, avoid making only minimum payments or utilising the full credit limit so you don't get caught in the debt trap.

WAYS TO AVOID A DEBT TRAP

1. Be aware of your financial health. Take note of your debt. Check the repayments being made and ensure that the principal amount of the loan is decreasing after every payment.

2. Make your payments regularly. Missing an EMI or credit card due will not only cost unnecessary

interest, but it will reduce your credit score as well (I explain what a credit score is in the next chapter). Try to automate your payments through auto-debit instructions. That way, your credit card dues will be automatically settled through your savings or salary account. Build an emergency fund to help you sustain economic shocks.

3. Consolidate loans if you are finding it hard to manage several debts. Consolidation will leave you with just one debt and one EMI. It will help you manage your money better.

4. Budget properly. Reduce expenditure to increase disposable income (the amount available with you that you can spend as per your will). This will help you to get rid of debt as soon as possible.

5. Pre-pay debt. A hike in your salary or your monthly income increases your debt-repaying capacity, so use that extra money to repay as much of your debt as possible. Sometimes prepayment may attract charges from the lender, but even then it will be worthwhile because it will help you reduce your interest burden.

6. Keep a track of your credit score as the interest rate on your future loans will increase with a decrease in your credit score.

How Much Should I Borrow?

10

This question is similar to deciding how much you should eat. The answer is simple—as much as you can digest healthily, because overeating will harm you. Borrowing or taking loans can provide you with a lavish lifestyle. If you can comfortably afford a holiday in Goa, taking a loan can offer you an opportunity to spend the vacation in Bali instead. Remember, just because you are eligible for credit doesn't mean that you can afford it.

What is the amount that you can actually afford to borrow? If your annual income is ₹6 lakhs, is it okay to borrow ₹4 lakhs to buy a car? Or, if your monthly income is ₹50,000, is it all right to have monthly debt repayments of ₹30,000?

CAR LOAN

I understand how important and exciting it is to buy the first car of your life. It is a critical milestone in a person's life. We compare and select the right type, right colour, suitability, brand, and so on. Along with it comes the hard work of getting it financed correctly—after all, we want the ride to be smooth.

While planning to take an auto loan, you should keep in mind the '20-4-10 rule'.

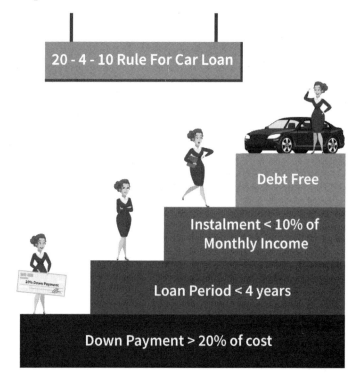

First of all, you should be able to pay at least 20% of the cost of the car as a down payment. This will reduce the interest cost and ultimately lower the cost of the vehicle for you. The higher the amount of down payment, the better your finances. And if you can't afford a suitable down payment, you are definitely looking at the wrong car. I have seen people fall into the no-down-payment trap, and end up with huge debts.

Secondly, keep in mind that the tenure of your loan should not exceed four years. Your lender may offer a longer tenure, but don't stretch the loan beyond four years. The shorter your loan period, the lower the interest you pay. Remember, a shorter tenure might come with a hefty monthly instalment, but it will hugely benefit your Personal Capital.

Thirdly, not more than 10% of your in-hand salary should be allocated for repaying the loan and car insurance. In-hand salary is your salary after all taxes and deductions. And this expense will form a part of your '30' from the 50-30-20 rule as discussed in the chapter on budgeting.

Apart from following the above rules, don't feel rushed to take a decision under the pressure of the dealers. Carefully compare quotes from different lenders. Don't focus on reducing the amount of EMIs but focus on getting a lower interest on the loan. Compare quotes by comparing total money outflows from your pocket.

HOW MUCH SHOULD MY TOTAL DEBT BE?

Apart from managing individual debts, you also have to keep a track of the total amount of outstanding debts and the total EMIs that are to be paid for various loans. This can be gauged excellently by the 20-10 rule. This rule aims to help you live your life within your means.

Total debt < 20% of yearly net income

EMI < 10% of monthly in-hand salary

20-10 Rule for Total Debt

Under this rule, you should make sure that your debt by the end of the year does not exceed 20% of your yearly post-tax net income, and the amount of your monthly instalments does not exceed 10% of your monthly in-hand salary. Now, it might be possible that due to some 'good loans', like an educational loan or a home loan, you are way above this threshold and you can do nothing about it. This is the time you should realise that you cannot afford new debts.

If you don't want to be a victim of a debt trap, you must be aware of your existing sources of income and your current expenditures. In addition, you should be ready for any contingencies. Now, you know that your annual income is one of the most critical factors in figuring out the maximum amount of loan that you can afford. But there are certain other factors that you should consider:

1. *Your fixed monthly financial obligations*: Sooner or later, you have to repay the debt along with the interest, possibly in monthly instalments. So, before taking up a loan, you should begin with noting down your fixed monthly expenditures like rent, school fees, electricity, other EMIs, and so on. This will help you figure out how much surplus you will have at the end of every month so that you can pay your instalments on time.

2. *Account for future uncertainties*: Even though you have a surplus remaining after providing for your monthly expenditures, don't forget to account for risks like a career break or a new commitment or any other problem that might affect your finances. However small your EMIs may be, ask yourself, what will happen if I lose my job? Don't forget, that even one bat can turn your life upside down (with reference to the Coronavirus).

DEBT REPAYMENT

Debt is an obstruction to your financial independence. It can be quite overwhelming to get rid of debt. Do you really need a strategy to pay off your debt? Well, this is just like asking 'Do you require a balm or medicine to cure your headache?' Of course you do, otherwise you'll have unwanted stress in life.

You need a strategy so that you can pay off the loans as soon as you can afford to. This will help you save yourself from being buried with interest costs. Any debt repayment strategy starts with prioritising your debt. You might be required to cut down certain expenditures for some time and make pocket-friendly choices, such as using public transport instead of cabs.

When it comes to paying off your debt, there are two main strategies:

The Avalanche Method

In this method, you pay the debt with the highest interest rate first. To begin with, categorise your debt in increasing order of interest. Then, start by paying off as much of the highest interest-charging debt while paying the minimum instalments on the rest. Once that debt is paid off, proceed with the next costliest debt, and so on.

This method is very helpful in preventing you from falling into debt traps and saves a lot of your money which would otherwise be paid as interest.

The Snowball Method

Although the avalanche method saves the most, the snowball method is preferred by many people as it keeps one motivated to get rid of the loan. This method is about getting rid of the smallest debt first. As soon as you see your loans getting cleared, you feel motivated by your small wins. So in this method, you start by listing your loans in the ascending order of amount outstanding. You have to begin by paying as much as you can of the smallest loan along with the minimum amount of other loans. After the smallest one is paid off, then move to the next.

Credit Score

11

I f you were living in a small village and the only option you had for borrowing money was going to a Lalaji or Sahukar, that is, the local moneylender, a credit score wouldn't be of much importance to you. But since you will need to go to a bank to borrow money, you'll require a good credit score. What is this credit score and why do banks consider it so important?

While giving out loans, banks and financial institutions face a risk of default by the borrower. So they require information about past borrowings and the borrower's track record regarding regularity in repayment. This information is provided in the form of a credit score by credit information companies. These companies collect, maintain and update records of all borrowings and repayments of individuals and business entities. Based on these records, they give a score called the 'credit score', and depending upon this credit score, financial institutions decide the approval, rejection and rate of interest for a loan. Thus, a credit score reflects your creditworthiness. So if you have taken any loan or if you possess a credit card, you too have a credit score.

There are four well-known credit information companies in India—Experian, TransUnion CIBIL, Highmark and Equifax. Out of these, TransUnion CIBIL is so popular that all credit scores are often called by the generic name 'CIBIL score'. CIBIL scores range between 300 and 900, where 900 denotes maximum creditworthiness. A CIBIL score of 750 or more is considered good. A score below that can make it harder for you to get financed. However, if you are planning to take a home loan, then you should have a score of at least 650. If you have no credit history, your score will be -1; once your credit history is at least six months old, your score will be 0.

Now, if you are planning to take a home loan in the future, I suggest you apply for a credit card (even if you don't need one), use it wisely (I repeat, wisely), and always pay before the due dates. This will help you to generate a credible credit history and make it easier to get a loan approved.

FACTORS DETERMINING YOUR CREDIT SCORE

Maintaining a good credit score is an integral part of personal finance. Even if you are not planning to take a loan, you never know when you will need a credit facility. Hence, you need to maintain your credit score all through your life. These are the factors that determine your credit score:

1. *Repayment History*: Depending on how regularly you pay your instalments when they are due, your repayment history is generated. It is given the highest weightage while determining your CIBIL score.

2. *Utilisation of Credit Balance*: One might feel that utilising the maximum balance of your credit

card could do no harm if the bill is paid on time. But the reality is, if you use the maximum credit limit sanctioned, it will adversely affect your credit score, and you will be considered as a risky borrower. So sometimes it is better to have two credit cards used at their 45% limits rather than one credit card used at its 90% limit.

3. *Duration of Credit or Loan*: The longer the period of your exposure to credit and its timely repayment, the better it will be for your CIBIL score.

4. *New Credits*: If you are applying for many credits from different institutions, it will adversely impact your credit score.

5. *Credit Mix*: This refers to your credit portfolio. Having only unsecured loans (such as personal loans) in your portfolio will reduce your credit score.

MAINTAINING YOUR CREDIT SCORE

1 *Pay off the Loan Balances*: Unpaid balances or dues on loans and credit cards may bring down your credit score. It's advisable to eliminate them.

2 *Check and Correct Your Credit Report*: You can quickly check your credit score online. It is essential to check your credit report. In this way, you can track which default is bringing your credit

score down, and if any incorrect information is reported about your credit score, you can get it corrected.

3　*Increase Your Credit Limit*: It is advisable to utilise only 30% of the credit limit offered. So to keep your credit utilisation ratio low, you can get the maximum limit of your credit card increased. But increasing the credit limit does not mean that you should spend more, so be careful about your spending.

4　*Manage Your Credit Cards Carefully*: This will include timely repayment by setting up payment reminders or e-mandates or auto-debits and consolidation of loans.

5　*Other Actions*: To maintain a good credit score, you might need to avoid:

a.　being a co-applicant or a guarantor of a loan for someone else when you need to borrow for yourself too,

b.　making too many loan applications in a short period, and

c.　having dormant credit cards lying around.

Module:
Investment

Investments: Do You Really Need Them?

12

When I was a kid, my dad used to explain to me how necessary it was to build a house with several pillars or columns. This was a vital element of any structure, which could help the house withstand any catastrophe. But do we construct a house with just one pillar? How much load can that one pillar take? What will happen if it is not able to survive an earthquake?

While planning to buy or construct a house, we analyse everything in detail—the size of the columns, their distancing and alignment and so forth. Similarly, why should you not analyse your current financial situation in detail? Just as you cannot make a strong and durable house based on just one pillar, you can't rely on just one source of income to help you sail through life.

Having a secure job is financial security, but having a recurring source of income through non-formal sources, enough to meet your monthly expenditures, is financial independence. Working forty to forty-five hours a week to earn your income isn't as interesting as sleeping comfortably in your bed and receiving money in your bank account. Yes, this is possible. You just have to put your money to the right use.

Remember the loop of wealth creation from Chapter 2?

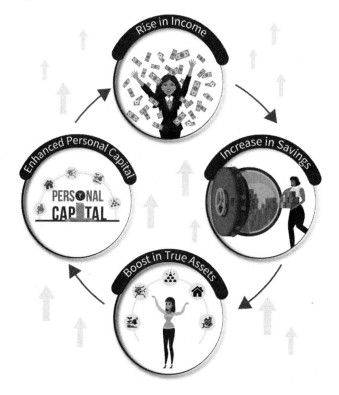

You can enter in this loop by channelizing savings in a way such that it increases your True Assets, which in turn raises your Personal Capital. This channelizing of savings is nothing but investment.

Your Personal Capital is something that works for you and earns money for you. An increase in your Personal Capital opens doors to new streams of income which, in turn, increase your savings. To harness the power of this loop of wealth creation, the only thing you need to do is invest your money in buying True Assets. If you are able to create a considerable amount of Personal Capital, you won't have to worry about fuelling the loop after retirement, as after some time, it takes care of itself.

Many people misunderstand investing as a mere tool to save taxes. A life insurance policy or contribution to your PF account will definitely help you save some taxes. But saving taxes should not be the sole criteria for an investment decision. The overall returns, in line with your objectives, should direct your decision-making

And saving tax is not enough. Investing possesses the power to provide you with inflation-beating returns and will enable you to harness the benefits of the loop of wealth creation. Your investment in True Assets will ensure that you meet all your goals at the right time. You should start focusing on investing proactively by buying True Assets. Otherwise, all your efforts will result in just trying to beat inflation, and not creating wealth, or enhancing your Personal Capital.

WHAT DRIVES THE LOOP OF WEALTH CREATION?

Remember 'compounding'? The factor that adversely affected the Personal Capital of Khushi and Tanya (when they took a loan), is the same wonder that drives the loop of wealth creation.

Suppose you invest ₹10,000 in a fixed deposit providing you a return of 7% per annum for 30 years. Every year you withdraw the interest earned. After the end of 30 years, your ₹10,000 will grow approximately three times to ₹31,000 (ignoring taxation). Now, with the same rate of interest, if you choose not to withdraw interest every year, the same sum of money will now grow more than seven times to ₹76,000.

This is the power of compounding. Through compounding, you earn money on money. For example, ₹10,000 invested today for an interest of 7% will grow to ₹10,700 in one year. If you decide to keep it invested, the interest on the second year will be earned on ₹10,700, providing you with ₹749 this time, and raising your investment amount to ₹11,449. If you again decide to keep this invested, you will earn interest on the entire ₹11,449, your initial corpus and interest earned over the years. Compounding earns you interest on interest, so your money grows manifold. All you need to do is stay invested and let compounding do the rest.

Khushi always knew that she had to focus on her Personal Capital. For her retirement, she started investing ₹5,000 every month in Mutual Funds via SIPs (systematic investment plans). Since the instalments were automatically deducted from her bank account, she never had to keep a track of the due dates. Tanya, on the other hand, was always too busy with her work. Whatever money she received was consumed for her household expenditures, and any excess money would be left in her savings account. By the time she turns fifty, Khushi would have invested a total of ₹15 lakhs in Mutual Funds over twenty-five years. Can you guess the amount of corpus she would accumulate?

You might be thinking that Khushi was depositing only ₹5,000 every month; that means only ₹60,000 per year. So, at most, her investment could double or triple and all she would end up with is ₹45 lakhs to ₹50 lakhs. Right? But what if I told you that her investment would grow over seven times in those twenty-five years? By the time she turns fifty, she would have a corpus of ₹95 lakhs (approximately) to plan her retirement (calculated at an average rate of return of 12% per annum).

Khushi started early, and because of that the small savings consistently made by her over a prolonged period were able to generate wealth for her. Anybody can unleash the power of compounding by starting early. You just need to have some patience, and then you'll see the money working for you. That's the reason Albert Einstein once described compounding as the 'eighth wonder of the world'. And, this 'wonder' fuels the loop of wealth creation.

What Are True Assets?

13

Personal finance starts with having a steady and recurring source of income. The source can be your salary or business, ensuring that you are able to meet your routine expenses. After that, you should plan for an emergency fund, a fund enough to support you at the time of any unforeseen events. Then comes the time to clear your debt—if not all debt, at least the high-interest debt. Finally, once you have added sufficient shock-absorbers to your finances, it is time you start buying True Assets.

I guess, from the beginning of this book, I have been talking about how these True Assets affect your life and your Personal Capital. What kind of investment options am I talking about?

Traditionally, people used to invest in gold, silver and land to save their money from inflation. In fact, these instruments provide satisfactory returns and are still preferred by many. All of them are tangible instruments, and investors feel safe as they can touch, see and feel their assets at any time.

REAL ESTATE

Real estate has been one of the most conventional and popular forms of investment. If you buy a house, the value will most probably increase with time; also, rents can be a great source of passive income. The returns generally vary from moderate to high.

If we talk about risks involved, there is the slight chance of a reduction in the value of assets. And, if you own a piece of land, there is the possibility of compulsory acquisition by the government. There are two major problems with a real estate investment. First of all, you need to invest a few lakhs. So you cannot utilise your small savings. Secondly, the investments have very low liquidity. It may take months to find a buyer at the right price. If the location of your property is too remote, there are chances that you might never find a buyer. Despite all this though, you can classify a real estate investment as your True Asset.

What about the house that you reside in? Many people tend to spend lavishly on their homes, considering it as a part of Personal Capital. Does that mean that buying an expensive house will increase your Personal Capital? What is the right approach to take?

HOME: AN ASSET OR A LIABILITY?

Buying a home is often considered as a milestone in our lives. A home is a dream for many while a necessity for all. How would you classify your house? Is it a True Asset? Ignore the emotions for some time and look at this from a sheer financial perspective.

Some people will classify it as a True Asset. After all, it is capable of generating cash flows if you sell or rent it. In fact, if you're living in your own house, you are saving cash outflows in the form of rent. In a developing country like India, where there is always scarcity of land and housing facilities due to population explosion, the value doesn't depreciate but only appreciates with time. Plus, you can mortgage it any time to get a secured loan.

The other way of looking at a house is to classify it as a liability as it demands additional fixed cash outflows in the form of maintenance and repair charges, municipal taxes, insurances, interest payment on home loans and such. The argument is that the value of the investment hardly appreciates, or even if it does, the returns do not beat inflation. However, in case of an adverse situation (such as job loss), it would be much better to possess a house rather than paying rent, as such cash outflows would hurt even more.

If you ask me, I would always consider buying land as an investment and would see land as a True Asset. Historically, land has provided substantial returns to its investors. I do find it hard to buy and sell, but it is a good investment option in India. When we talk about classification of a house as a True Asset or not, it totally depends on the type of property.

Today, when you buy real estate, you do not buy only the land and the house. The real estate project comes with amenities like club houses, gardens, play areas, auditorium facilities, swimming pools, and so on. This means that you are not just investing in a real estate project by buying a home, you are buying an experience. Your home is now more than just land and a building.

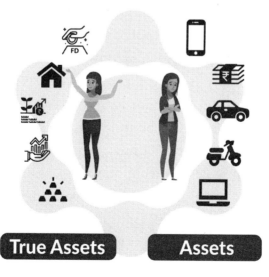

True Assets   **Assets**

The experience, which you are buying along with your real estate investment, doesn't count as an investment; rather it's an expenditure. The more amenities you add, the more expensive your house will be. It will also raise your monthly maintenance expenditure. In such a scenario, you cannot classify your house as a True Asset. So before classifying your house as a True Asset, figure out what you are actually paying for.

OTHER FORMS OF TRUE ASSETS

When it comes to metals like gold and silver, they have been the most trusted form of investments in India, though they come with the problem of storage, as theft is a major risk. Prices might fluctuate, but gold has been successful in providing moderate returns through capital appreciation to its investors. It is not capable of providing any passive income, but the liquidity is quite high. You can easily find a buyer and the minimum amount of investment can be low; thus it can be used for investing small amounts. Personally, I think, one should avoid investing in gold via gold jewellery, as making charges and other associated costs can bring down your return. Bullion and coins can be a better way, but, in my opinion, the best way to invest in gold is sovereign gold bonds issued by the RBI, where you don't have to be worried about storage costs or theft, and yet, at the same time, you can take advantage of the appreciation of the metal. Sovereign gold bonds not only derive their value from gold and appreciate along with it, they also provide an interest of 2.5% per annum that can serve as a steady passive income for the investor.

Another traditional form of a True Asset is fixed deposits, which can be a good avenue to park your emergency fund, but is not capable of generating stupendous returns.

UNVEILING EQUITY INVESTMENT

Do you ever dream of owning a business but hesitate due to a lack of expertise, funds and time? Well, in that case, one brilliant form of investment can be equity shares, where you can invest directly in any of the companies listed on the stock exchange. Once you buy an equity share, you get the proportionate ownership of that company, and you have a right to share the profits, you get a right to vote, and as the company grows, you also get a capital appreciation on your investment. Investment in equity shares can be used to mobilise savings as low as ₹100, with a potential of growing them multiple times. Do you know that an investment of ₹10,000 in Infosys in 1993 would have grown to ₹2,97,30,645 by 2017? That's a 2,973 times growth.

Just as there are risks involved in business, equity investments are considered quite risky. This risk can surely be reduced but cannot be eliminated.

Another form of investment is Mutual Funds. A Mutual Fund is like an investment vehicle which invests in underlying assets such as stocks, bonds, other Mutual Funds or any other asset. Mutual Funds come in a variety of options depending on the asset they invest in. For example, a Mutual Funds investing in equity shares of companies are classified as equity-oriented Mutual Funds. Similarly, Mutual Funds investing in debt instruments are called debt-oriented Mutual Funds. So by investing in a Mutual Fund, you indirectly invest in all the companies that the Fund has invested in. They are preferred for their liquidity and hence considered as a convenient form of investment. They are perfect to mobilise your small monthly savings, with a potential of providing returns that can not only beat inflation but also create wealth for you. The investment is subjected to risk levels from low to high, depending on the type of Mutual Fund.

CRITERIA FOR MAKING INVESTMENT
CHOICES: DIVERSIFICATION AND ALLOCATION

I have met people who invested their life's savings into equity just to get rich, and have lost it all! Since investment in the stock market is considered as the riskiest form of investment, the amount of risk that one should take should reduce with age. Thus, as you get older, I suggest that you minimise your equity investments. As a thumb rule, you take the number 100 and subtract your age from it. The result should be your *maximum* equity allocation. This means if you are 20, you can invest a maximum of 80% of corpus into equity shares and equity-oriented Mutual Funds.

The bottom line is, you need to select the right investment instrument for yourself based on your investment amount, risk tolerance, returns required and goals. Remember, don't put all your eggs in one basket. Diversify your investments using various instruments.

If you are considering putting all your money into real estate, read about the United States' 'housing bubble' leading to a crash in the market. If you are thinking that FDs are the safest option, then don't forget that their post-tax returns might not be able to beat inflation, and there is always a chance of bank default (although a very rare scenario). Similarly, stock markets and Mutual Funds are subjected to market risks. I suggest that you should invest in a properly balanced portfolio consisting of different investment instruments.

Retirement Planning

14

Regardless of your age, your gender or the number of dependents, there is one common goal for every individual—retirement planning. Now, some of you might feel that you are too young to think about retirement. It is something that can wait or be considered later. Well, do you know, as I write this in 2020, the average age of Indians is around twenty-nine. Around 50% of India's population is below the age of twenty-five and 65% is below thirty-five. This means, the majority of the population is in a position to work to make their ends meet. But what will happen after twenty-five years? By 2045, this working population will be on the verge of retirement. Do you think that our country will be ready to provide for the majority of the population in twenty-five years? Do you still think it is something that's not worthy of being given a thought now?

Earlier, I told you that Khushi expects to make around ₹95 lakhs by investing ₹5,000 per month for twenty-five years (her own total investment being ₹15 lakh). On the other hand, Tanya started planning for retirement much later. She started investing ₹20,000 per month only when she was thirty-six. This means that by the time she is fifty, she would have invested around ₹33 lakhs (more than double of what Khushi invested). But still, at the time of redemption, when she is fifty (at the same average return of 12%), her corpus will be around ₹87 lakhs.

This difference is again explained by the compounding of money, where small sums, when invested over a prolonged period, generate large wealth for the investor.

SAB
MOH
MAYA
HAI

Thus, whenever someone asks me, 'When should I start planning for my retirement?' I say, 'Do it now!' Many people say that they do not invest as investing is risky. In my opinion, not having sufficient money when required is riskier. Why should you not live life to the fullest? If you are concerned about market risks, start early. By starting as early you can, you have sufficient time to learn. Risk and reward go hand-in-hand in investing. Higher the risk, higher the return. If you stay invested, the lower your risks will be. For example, no one can forecast how the stock market will behave over the next week or month or even a year. But, one can be certain that over the next ten years, it will be higher, and over the next twenty years, still higher.

RETIREMENT PLANS AND SCHEMES

To support the large size of the ageing population in the future, the Indian government is creating awareness about retirement planning and, over the years, has launched various schemes such as the National Pension Scheme (NPS), Atal Pension Yojana (APY), and Public Provident Fund (PPF). To encourage investments, these instruments also provide some tax benefits to the investor. Investment in any of these instruments will form a part of your Personal Capital. Let's have a look at them.

National Pension Scheme

The National Pension Scheme (NPS) is a tool for retirement planning offered by the government of India. It was launched in 2004. Earlier, it was limited to government employees only, but in 2009 it was opened to all. The objective of this scheme is to provide regular income to citizens when they stop working. All you need to do is deposit an amount regularly and get the benefits of compounding on the returns. Upon maturity, you can withdraw a part of the amount as a lump sum, and the remaining can be used to buy an annuity. Any Indian citizen between the age of eighteen to sixty-five can subscribe to NPS.

NPS offers two types of accounts—tier-I and tier-II, where the former is mandatory for all and the latter is voluntary. Tier-I accounts have a strict rule of no withdrawal. You cannot withdraw any money until you reach sixty years of age or you retire from your job. The minimum contribution required in the tier-I account is ₹500 per month, while minimum annual contribution should be ₹1,000. In case of the tier-II account, if you choose to contribute, the minimum amount has to be ₹250. In case the subscriber does not make a specified minimum contribution, the account will be frozen and can be reactivated by paying the required amount with a nominal fine of ₹100. In case of emergencies before retirement, you are allowed to withdraw up to 25% of the deposited amount if you have contributed for three years or more in a tier-I account. The tier-II account has no such limitation on deposit and withdrawal (with some exceptions for government employees). A unique Permanent Retirement Account Number (PRAN) is issued to each subscriber and no individual can have more than one account.

In NPS, you can decide the allocation of your investment into debt (government, corporate) and equity instruments based on your risk appetite. By following the general rule of investment of '100 minus your age', you can decide this allocation. This means that if your current age is twenty-five, then you can allocate 25% of funds in debt instruments and the remaining 75% in equity schemes. If you do not want to follow this rule or don't know how to do it, don't worry at all. Our government took care of such technicalities and offered a feature of auto allocation of funds. If you are young, say around twenty-five, then the system will allocate more than 50% of funds for equity and the remaining for debt instruments. Year after year, this percentage of allocation for equity will keep on decreasing and allocation for debt instruments will keep on increasing.

You can invest a lump-sum amount or make a monthly deposit as per your convenience. There are entities called Point of Presence Service Providers (POP–SPs) who are authorised to provide the facility of NPS subscription.

NPS gives the flexibility to switch POPs twice a year as per your choice. There are around fifty-eight POPs, which includes banks, both private and public sector, and other financial institutions. You can locate your nearest POP through the website of the Pension Fund Regulatory and Development Authority (PFRDA). Also, you can subscribe online through eNPS. You can get all the required details and guidelines on the website of National Securities Depository Services Limited (NSDL).

Apart from wealth creation, you get income tax benefits under section 80CCD (1B) and 80C of the Income Tax Act. The maximum deduction is ₹1.5 lakhs under section 80C and an additional benefit of ₹50,000 under 80CCD(1B). In this way, you can save tax on ₹2 lakhs if you completely utilise this provision. However, no tax deductions can be claimed if you invest in a tier-II account.

Also, you get to enjoy tax benefits at the time of retirement. Presently, the subscriber has the option to withdraw up to 60% of the total accumulated funds as a lump-sum amount (without paying any taxes) and use the remaining 40% to purchase an annuity. Pensions received from annuity will be taxed in slab rates.

Here's a scenario explaining how this scheme can benefit you. Suppose you start investing ₹1,000 per month in NPS. You deposit ₹1,000 for the next thirty-five years and will not be able to withdraw any money. Overall, you will invest a total of ₹4,20,000 until you turn sixty. Assuming the return on investment to be 10%, your wealth will be around ₹40 lakhs.

On retirement at the age of sixty, you could choose to withdraw 40% as a lump sum and, from the remaining 60%, you can purchase an annuity for the next twenty years, with a monthly payout.

Out of the pension wealth of around ₹40 lakhs, you will get ₹16 lakhs, without any tax deduction. The remaining ₹24 lakhs will be received as ₹16,500 per month for the next twenty years.

So even if you're not aware of the intricacies of the financial world, you can save enough for your retirement simply by starting early. Every year you would have deposited ₹12,000, which will give you an additional tax benefit (given the limit of ₹50,000 in NPS). Just by investing ₹4.2 lakhs in small amounts, you can generate an enormous wealth of ₹40 lakhs. In addition, you will not have to pay any tax on the ₹16 lakhs received as a lump-sum amount at the time of retirement.

The Indian government has been trying to make the scheme more and more attractive. It may be possible that the lump-sum withdrawal limit is increased, offering higher benefits to investors.

Summary of the benefits of NPS:

- Auto-allocation of funds
- Tax benefit under section 80CCD
- Higher returns than other pension schemes
- The convenience of subscribing, managing and withdrawals online
- No exit load

The only disadvantage of this scheme is the lock-in period. You cannot withdraw until the retirement age. Yes, it can be a problem if you need that money in between because the investment horizon is quite long. However, if you are a spendthrift, then this may prove to be a good feature. As the name suggests, the scheme was solely devised for retirement purposes only. If the flexibility of withdrawal is given, then people will withdraw in case of emergency and regret later at the time of retirement. So this disadvantage may actually prove to be a big advantage as it guarantees the availability of funds when you stop working.

Atal Pension Yojana

The Atal Pension Yojana (APY) is another scheme offered by the government of India to provide a fixed pension to its citizens, especially in the unorganised sector. The subscriber is guaranteed to receive a monthly pension ranging from ₹1,000 to ₹5,000 based on the plan chosen. This scheme is administered by the Pension Fund Regulatory and Development Authority (PFRDA), a government agency, and is implemented through banks. Any person between eighteen and forty years of age with a savings account can subscribe to this scheme. A subscriber needs to contribute until the age of sixty. You have the option of receiving a monthly pension between ₹1,000 and ₹5,000, in units of ₹1,000. Based on your option and current age, your premium amount is decided. Younger individuals need to pay less. Therefore, the monthly premium amount may vary in the range of ₹42 to ₹1,318 based on your age and monthly requirements. There is a penalty slab linked to it in cases of delayed payments which ranges from ₹1 to ₹10 based on your monthly premium.

As per your comfort level and capacity, you have the option of selecting your instalment frequency. There is an auto-debit facility as well. So you just have to identify your requirements and accordingly subscribe to the scheme and the rest will be taken care of automatically. You can exit before maturity only in exceptional circumstances. Also, just like NPS, you are entitled to tax exemption under section 80CCD (1B) of the Income Tax Act, which provides an additional limit of ₹50,000 apart from the ₹1.5 lakhs exemption offered under section 80C.

Public Provident Fund (PPF)

Public Provident Fund (PPF) is another scheme offered by the government of India and is good for individuals who are risk averse in nature. It is a risk-free investment option as returns are guaranteed by the government. Also, the funds invested in PPF are not linked to market performance. Therefore, it can provide stable returns over a long period.

Any Indian citizen can open a PPF account. But a joint account is not allowed. Even minors can open this account as long as there is a guardian to operate it. Unlike NPS, non-resident Indians (NRIs) are not allowed to have a PPF account. This scheme comes with a lock-in period of fifteen years, so you cannot withdraw any funds before the account matures in fifteen years. On the other hand, if you do not require the funds after fifteen years, then you have the option of extending the tenure in blocks of five years. However, in emergencies, you are allowed to withdraw some amount or take a loan under certain conditions.

The subscriber has to deposit a minimum amount of ₹500 every year and can deposit a maximum of ₹1.5 lakhs annually. Deposits can be made as per the user's convenience, either in yearly or monthly instalments. Every year some amount has to be deposited to ensure the active status of the account.

The returns or interest payments are determined by the government of India, and the rate is generally higher than normal savings accounts. The interest rate applicable is updated on a quarterly basis. Apart from the assured interest, you are entitled to enjoy the benefits of tax exemptions under section 80C of the Income Tax Act of 1961. You can claim a tax waiver on the entire amount deposited during the year. The total interest earned during the year is exempt from tax. Also, the subscriber does not have to pay any tax on the entire corpus upon maturity. These features of PPF make it more attractive and motivates people to invest and plan their retirement.

The following are some of the major benefits under PPF:

- Risk-free investment
- Tax benefit on investment
- No tax on the maturity amount
- Lock-in period is just fifteen years
- Can be easily managed online

Apart from the schemes discussed above, there are certain other retirement plans as well, offered by private players. If you do not want to invest in pension funds or want to further diversify your investments, then you've got other viable options for long-term growth, such as Mutual Funds.

Mutual Funds

15

The first thing that would probably come to your mind in case of Mutual Funds is the oft-repeated disclaimer, 'Mutual Funds are subjected to market risk. Read all scheme-related documents carefully before investing.' And they are usually promoted as *'Mutual Funds sahi hain* (Mutual Funds are correct)'. They possess the maximum potential to positively impact your Personal Capital.

And why do I say so? Because I've seen Khushi reaping the fruits of Mutual Fund investments. Remember, she always saved at least 20% of her salary? She used to invest this amount in Mutual Funds. Recently, she was able to buy a lavish house for herself from the corpus that she had generated from her small SIPs. On the other hand, Tanya is struggling to get a home loan and get a nice house for herself. That's the difference a Mutual Fund investment can create.

Mutual Fund, as the term suggests, is a collection of funds mutually contributed by investors for a common purpose. Generally, the money collected is invested in a pool of instruments such as stocks, bonds, gold and other similar assets. These funds are operated and managed by fund managers, who manage the underlying assets in such a manner as to produce maximum gains. A Mutual Fund is driven by a predetermined, pre-announced investment objective or mandate.

Assume that there is a Mutual Fund company that collects funds from 100 investors who contribute ₹500 each making a total corpus of ₹50,000. With this corpus, the company buys twenty shares of ₹2,500 each. Now these twenty shares cannot be distributed among all 100 contributors. So, the fund manager creates a scheme and issues units which can be distributed among the contributors proportionately. Every unit derives its value from the underlying investments in instruments (shares, in this case). The value of each unit of a Mutual Fund is referred to as the Net Asset Value (NAV).

NAV can be simply understood as a sort of a purchase or selling price for Mutual Funds. Just like how we have buying and selling prices of goods and services, a Mutual Fund unit can be bought or sold for a price that is equal to its NAV. The NAV keeps on changing with the changes in the prices of the underlying assets and is updated at the close of each trading day.

HOW ARE MUTUAL FUNDS AND STOCK MARKETS RELATED?

The best way to invest in the share market with the least risk is through Mutual Funds. Warren Buffett, one of the world's greatest investors, has advised that one should never put all one's eggs in one basket. We cannot be sure about any company's future. It can be a company like Kingfisher Airlines which went bankrupt, or it can be like Reliance Industries which has been able to give manifold returns. Therefore, you must invest in various companies or investment instruments because if any of them turns out to be a loss-making deal, then you can rely on profits from other investments. But again, what if all your selected stocks are not performing well? Don't worry, there is a solution to every problem. If you do not have enough knowledge about the functioning of markets, do not have technical skills, or do not have time to do proper research for investment, you can easily rely on Mutual Funds.

Suppose you own a car and you know how to drive it. You will still have two options: either you drive on your own to reach the destination and enjoy the ride, or you could hire a driver. With a driver, you don't have to worry about the road, traffic, stops, and such. All decisions, such as how fast to drive, which route to take, and where to stop, will be made by the hired professional. This is the difference between trading in the stock market yourself and investing in Mutual Funds. In Mutual Funds, there is a fund manager who makes all the decisions for you regarding which instruments to buy, how much of each instrument to buy, and other such intermediate decisions, at a nominal fee. All you have to do is just buy the units of a Mutual Fund based on your investment objectives and time horizon.

WHY MUTUAL FUNDS?

The best way to invest in the share market for people who don't understand its intricacies is through Mutual Funds.

Mutual Funds are the perfectly-balanced investment instruments with respect to the 'risk and rewards'. Therefore, to fulfil your medium to long-term financial goals (be it children's education, marriage, a dream vacation or whatever), this could prove to be the most crucial part of your Personal Capital.

You just need to identify your requirements and time horizon, and select a fund that can meet your investment objectives. All the decisions related to identification, purchase and selling of specific shares or bonds are taken by the fund managers, who are experienced experts in their fields. The benefits of investing in Mutual Funds are below:

Diversification

You can easily diversify your portfolio as there are Mutual Funds for a variety of assets. This helps in reducing risk to a great extent.

Liquidity

Mutual Funds can be redeemed easily. Whenever you need the funds, you can submit a redemption request for a part or all of your investment and you can receive the funds in your bank account within one to three days, depending on the type of the Mutual Fund.

Economies of Scale

Creating a diverse portfolio requires many transactions. For each type of instrument that you want to invest in, you need to make a separate transaction. There is a fee associated with each transaction which will add up to huge costs if you want a well-diversified portfolio. This problem is easily solved by Mutual Funds, because they buy and sell large quantities of securities at a time, which reduces transaction costs.

Professional Management

The biggest advantage of a Mutual Fund is the professional management by knowledgeable fund managers. They do all the research to identify potential investment avenues and allocate funds accordingly. If you are a beginner or do not have sufficient knowledge about the functioning of capital markets, then investing in Mutual Funds is the best option since your money is managed by professionals at a nominal fee. The fund companies manage all administrative activities and compliances.

Transparency

This is the most essential factor in order to gain customers' trust. This is achieved by the presence of regulators like the Securities and Exchange Board of India (SEBI). All the information related to Mutual Funds is available on various online platforms and company websites. The accounting and reporting of the valuation of the investment portfolios are done on a regular basis.

A Variety of Choices

Different Mutual Fund managers follow different styles and strategies to design an investment portfolio according to different goals. The strategies can be value investing, growth investing, low-risk investing, among others. You have the freedom to select any of these funds after proper research and evaluation.

I have observed that even after I am successful in motivating people to start focusing on Personal Capital, and they are finally about to invest, the jargon and terminologies used by some experts come in the way. They start getting confused about what type of Mutual Fund to select, what are the pros and cons, if their evaluation methodology is correct, and so on. So, to address this, I will explain Mutual Funds in some more detail.

DIRECT AND REGULAR PLANS

There are two types of plans through which you could invest in a Mutual Fund—direct and regular plans. You can buy the direct plan from the Mutual

Fund or from selected websites. The regular plan can be bought through an agent, like a broker or distributor. The only difference between these two is that, in regular plans, the Asset Management Company (AMC), that is, the Mutual Fund company, will deduct some amount from your returns and pay it as a commission to the investment advisor, broker or distributor through whom you purchased the Mutual Fund units.

My Opinion

I would recommend a direct plan because you will get higher returns as there is no intermediary commission. By opting for a regular plan, a part of your investment corpus will be given out as commission to the agent, which will reduce your overall return from investment.

TYPES OF MUTUAL FUNDS

Based on Flexibility

Open-Ended Funds

In Open-Ended Funds, there are no restrictions on the holding period and investors can enter or exit at any time. There are also no restrictions on the number of units to be bought or sold. There is no fixed maturity date and you can trade units at the prevailing NAV at any time. Because of this flexibility and the convenience it provides to an investor, these are the most preferred funds.

Closed-Ended Funds

They have a predefined maturity period and you can invest in them only during the initial offer period. You cannot enter into such schemes after that and are not allowed to exit before maturity. In some cases, these funds are listed on the stock exchange, but the transaction volumes are usually very small.

Interval Funds

Interval funds carry characteristics of both open-ended and Closed-Ended Funds. You can enter and redeem such funds only at predefined intervals as decided by the fund house. These funds are good for people who have short-term financial goals.

My Opinion

I prefer to invest in an Open-Ended Mutual Fund. Open-Ended funds provide liquidity as investors can withdraw funds when needed. Also, in Close-Ended funds, one has to invest in lump sum. They cannot be used as a tool to create discipline to save every month and mobilise small savings. Lastly, an Open-Ended scheme also provides investors with a track record of performance, enabling them to make informed decisions.

Based on Asset Classes

Equity-Oriented Mutual Funds

As the name suggests, equity-oriented Mutual Funds invest their funds predominantly in equity shares of companies. The fund managers scan the market and, after thorough research, identify some shares which can give returns as per the scheme's objectives. Generally, investments are made in companies from different sectors. This diversification is done to reduce the risk associated with market fluctuations. These Mutual Funds can be high risk and volatile, because they invest in stocks and other equity instruments such as market indices. They have the potential to give higher returns but can give high losses as well because their returns depend on the performance of the stock market. But if you are looking to invest for a longer period, then you should definitely go ahead with Equity Funds.

The companies listed on the stock exchange are classified as Large-Cap, Mid-Cap and Small-Cap companies. This classification is done on the basis of their market capitalisation (valuation of a company based on current market price) as follows:

- Large-Cap: Top 100 companies in terms of market capitalisation
- Mid-Cap: 101st–250th companies in term of market capitalisation
- Small-Cap: 251st company onwards in terms of market capitalisation

The companies in the Large-Cap segment have high market capitalisation and are in the maturity stage. They are treated as more stable and reliable as compared to Mid-Cap and Small-Cap companies. The Mid-Cap and Small-Cap companies are considered to be in the growth and inception phase respectively and have a higher growth potential along with higher risks.

An Equity Fund can have shares of many companies spread across these segments. SEBI, the regulator, has allowed fund houses to create eleven categories of funds based on these distinctions. It can be a Large-Cap Fund where the majority of fund allocation goes to Large-Cap companies. Similarly, there can be Mid-Cap Funds, Small-Cap Funds, Multi-Cap Funds. The Multi-Cap Funds have pre-defined proportions of Large-Cap, Mid-Cap and Small-Cap companies, depending on the scheme objectives. Equity Funds can further be classified as follows:

An Equity Linked Savings Scheme (ELSS) is a special type of Equity Fund. The amount invested in this fund would be deducted from your total taxable income up to a limit of ₹1.5 lakhs under section 80C of the Income Tax Act 1961. However, there is a lock-in period. You cannot redeem your units for a period of three years from the date of allotment of units.

Debt Funds

Debt Funds invest in the debt securities issued by corporates and the government. These include bonds, debentures and commercial papers. When an investor buys such instruments, it means they are lending money to the issuer of the debt for a certain period in exchange for a fixed interest. Such funds are ideal for risk-averse investors, who are satisfied with lower but fixed returns. Debt Funds are most suited for short-term goals, or if you want to park your money for a short duration but earn better interest than from a savings account.

Based on the type of security and time horizon, Debt Funds can be further classified:

Balanced or Hybrid Funds

Mutual Funds with debt and equity instruments in different proportions are called hybrid funds. The objective behind such funds is to diversify your portfolio and reduce your exposure to market risks by investing in varied assets. Some hybrid funds have a fixed allocation of assets, while others provide flexibility to investors, allowing them to allocate based on their requirements. These funds are suitable for investors with a moderate risk appetite.

Solution-Oriented Funds

Solution-oriented schemes are the types of Mutual Funds whose portfolios are designed to meet specific financial goals. Such schemes are better suited for investors with specific goals or investors who want to create wealth for financial goals such as marriage, retirement or children's education. The fund managers create solution-oriented schemes tailored according to the goal, expected return, and risk aptitude of investors. These schemes come with a lock-in period and exit load structure as decided by a fund house. Such schemes can act as a proxy for the National Pension Scheme (NPS) that is offered as a retirement planning tool. If you do not want to wait until retirement or want a more customised plan, then you can opt for solution-oriented funds with a systematic withdrawal plan as per your needs.

Other Funds

All other funds apart from those mentioned above come under this category. It is nothing but a different combination of assets in a portfolio. Some of these are listed below:

- Emerging market fund
- Fund of funds
- International/foreign fund

- Global fund
- Gold Mutual Fund
- Real estate fund

There are hundreds of funds available in the market with different combinations of equity and debt instruments in various ratios. It becomes extremely challenging for an individual to choose from these many options. The key here is long-term investment and deciding to invest as early as possible. If you choose carefully, any fund can give a better return on investment than traditional money market instruments.

My Opinion

Debt Funds are not completely risk-free, especially since rising defaults have been a problem since the last few years.

Balanced fund managers charge a higher fee for these funds compared to the returns they provide. Consider the following funds along with the management fee:

Type of Fund	Name of Fund	Fee
Equity Fund	ICICI Prudential Value Discovery Fund	1.85%
Debt Fund	ICICI Prudential Bond Fund	0.56%
Balanced Fund	ICICI Prudential Balanced Advantage Fund	1.74%

Fund houses generally charge a higher management fee for Equity Funds due to the complexity of the work involved. ICICI Balanced Fund has invested almost half its funds in debt instruments, and the fee charged is almost equal to that of the Equity Fund. Also, currently, the taxes on long-term capital gains on equity-oriented Mutual Funds are way less than that of Debt Funds. Thus, I feel Equity Funds will provide better post-tax returns when compared to debt or Balanced Funds.

Generally, equity markets provide a compounded annual growth rate of 10–12%. This means that even if you stay invested in Index Funds, you could conveniently grow your money at an average rate of 10%. However, equity-oriented Mutual Funds have the potential to provide returns ranging from 12% to 18% on investment.

How Can You Invest in Mutual Funds?

16

There are two major ways of investing in any Mutual Fund—systematic investment plan (SIP) and lump-sum investment. If you opt for SIP, you can invest small amounts at regular intervals, such as monthly or quarterly. The investment amount will be directly deducted from your bank account, so you won't have to go through the trouble of making the payment every time. You are generally given an option to stop any time you want, and there are no extra charges if you miss an instalment.

On the other hand, investing a lump sum means making a one-time, bulk investment. Even if you are investing a lump sum, the minimum amount of investment can be as low as ₹1,000 (it is different for different funds).

My Opinion

In my opinion, SIP is a great option to invest regularly. Since the amount gets automatically deducted, investors do not bother altering the procedure, and end up creating substantial Personal Capital for themselves. Investing via SIPs averages out the fluctuations in purchase price due to market fluctuations. It also inculcates a habit of disciplined saving in investors.

A lump-sum investment can also be opted for if you have received a substantial one-time amount. But I prefer making a lump-sum investment in a Mutual Fund only after analysing the market thoroughly, so that I do not end up buying the units at an expensive price.

SYSTEMATIC WITHDRAWAL PLAN

Systematic Withdrawal Plan (SWP) is a feature used for withdrawing an amount from your Mutual Fund on a periodic basis. Investors can withdraw a specific amount of payout or redeem a specific number of units at a predetermined interval, like monthly, quarterly, half-yearly or annually. Investors can use this feature to meet their routine needs.

When Should You Opt for SWP?

Investors can opt for this feature in order to meet monthly or routine expenditures. Only the number of units corresponding to the amount required are redeemed, and the rest continue to be invested.

PARAMETERS TO CONSIDER BEFORE BUYING FUNDS

All the information related to a Mutual Fund is available in the fact sheet provided by the AMCs. Also, there is a lot of useful information available on online platforms, where you can directly compare funds of your choice. The following are some of the important parameters that you must check before making a purchase decision:

Risk Profile

The risk-bearing capacity is different for every individual, depending on the number of dependents, age, fixed obligations and such. Thus, before buying any Mutual Fund, make sure it fits your risk profile. Generally, we consider Large-Cap Mutual Funds as safer options as the companies are in a maturity stage of the business cycle. On the other hand, Small-caps are mostly the newer companies, which might get adversely affected by even small changes in market conditions. So don't forget to consider your risk appetite before investing.

Asset Under Management (AUM)

AUM is the value of assets that the fund house is handling on behalf of investors. The size of the AUM has a direct relation to the popularity of the fund in the market. A higher AUM means more investors have invested more money in the fund. AUM also has an impact on total expenses of the fund. A fixed percentage of commission is levied on the total AUM, which the fund management charges. If there are more unit holders in a given fund, then usually the expenses per unit holder decreases. But remember, large AUMs also means slower reactions to changes in market conditions and hence lower returns for investors. So whenever you are opting for a Small-Cap or Mid-Cap Fund, look for funds with lower AUM; in all other cases, the higher the AUM, the better it is.

Expense Ratio

While providing services to investors, the AMC charges a certain annual maintenance fee. This includes operating costs, administrative costs and advertisement expenses. The expense ratio is calculated by dividing these expenses by AUM. A higher expense ratio would reduce your return. Expense ratio differs from fund to fund. For example, it is lower for Index Funds and higher for Active Funds. This is because an active fund reflects the skill set and knowledge of the fund manager, while with an Index Fund, the fund manager only replicates the index without any research. So, if you feel that your actively managed fund has outperformed the benchmark, then there is no harm in giving a little extra money to the fund manager. The same applies to a Debt Fund, where the expense ratio should be less, as it does not require much research. It varies from fund house to fund house and is also known as Management Expense Ratio (MER). It should be as low as possible.

Portfolio Turnover Ratio (PTR)

This indicates the frequency of changes in fund holdings. It gives an idea about the strategy followed by the fund manager to generate expected returns. PTR can be calculated by dividing the value of securities bought or sold by average net assets. If PTR is high, then it means the fund manager is following the trading strategy which will increase the transaction cost and thereby reduce returns. A low PTR, on the other hand, means that the fund manager is following a buy and hold strategy. Compare PTR with returns. A high PTR is justified with high returns.

Fund Manager Track Record

The performance of a Mutual Fund largely depends on the fund manager, the ultimate decision maker. So it is imperative to analyse the track record of the fund manager. This can be done by reviewing the performance of the past returns of funds managed by them and comparing the returns with the set benchmark as well as other Mutual Funds in the same category.

Fund House Systems and Reputation

The systems and the checks and controls of the AMC will determine the safety of your investments and provide consistent returns. An unknown fund house may give high returns for a short period but subsequently collapse since they did not have proper systems or the fund manager took inappropriate risks.

Exit Load

This is the fee charged by the Mutual Fund if investors redeem their units before a specified period. The primary reason for levying this charge is because the nature of the scheme requires staying invested for a certain period before adequate returns can be expected. Exit load varies across different Mutual Fund schemes. Always factor in the exit load before taking a decision.

Performance Comparison

There are a number of AMCs in India that offer different types of funds, so it is important to compare the performance with peers and benchmark returns to identify a suitable fund. You can list down similar schemes and compare their returns for different periods such as the returns for the last quarter, six months, twelve months, three years, and five years.

However, always remember that past returns are no indication of what will happen in the future. You need to evaluate what changes are likely to occur that will impact the performance of different categories and kinds of Mutual Funds and other investment avenues.

Module:
Taxation

Introduction to Taxes

17

You must be familiar with taxes, and they need no introduction. But in this module, we are going to introduce you to the real face of taxation. It's possible that you may not be aware of it. Here's an example for you that may blow your mind.

Imagine it's your day off and you decide to cook for your family. Your family members are quite excited about it, and you happily wear the apron to see that smile on their faces. Of course, you are not a trained chef, and therefore you toil hard in the kitchen for hours. After all the hard work, the dish is finally ready. Your family is amazed by the smell of the dish and all of you are ready to grab a piece of it.

But wait! Just as you are about to enjoy a piece of it, a government representative storms into your house and claims a part of the dish, saying that a part of your meal belongs to the government and you can't consume it fully. Shocked and hungry, you look at the annoyed faces of your family members. All your excitement is shattered just because the government has claimed that a part of the dish belongs to them. Wouldn't you be angry about your hard work going in vain? That's the ugly side of taxation that you may not be aware of. But it's undoubtedly imperative for you to know.

Do you know how much tax you pay to the government?

If you are a salaried individual, you must be aware of the tax deducted from your salary. The taxation doesn't end there. If you are thinking that you are paying 30% of your income to the government, you are wrong! You are paying way more than that. Taxes are more pervasive than you think.

Let's say your gross salary is ₹1 lakh per month. After taking the benefit of various deductions, suppose you are required to pay 15% income tax, that is, ₹15,000.

Now, with the remaining ₹85,000, you decide to buy a scooter. The ex-showroom price quoted to you is ₹66,000. This price is inclusive of 28% GST (goods and service tax). GST is an indirect tax. Thus, while buying a scooter (without any accessories), you are paying almost ₹14,400 as tax to the government.

The next step after buying a vehicle is getting it registered with the regional transport office (RTO) after paying the registration tax (road tax). The tax generally varies between 2% and 10% of the cost of a vehicle (the ex-showroom price). Thus, the road tax paid to the government may be around ₹3,500.

Till now, out of your salary of ₹1 lakh, you have paid the government income tax, GST and road tax, all amounting to ₹42,900. And if you decide to buy accessories for your vehicle, be ready to pay more GST. We have not taken into account insurance, on which the applicable GST is currently 18%.

Now, the scooter won't run by itself. You will need petrol. Around 69% of the cost of petrol is taxes. Thus, if you are buying 5 litres of petrol at ₹70 per litre, your cash outflow will be ₹350, out of which approximately ₹240 is paid to the government. Think about the quantity of petrol you are going to put in your vehicle and the taxes you are about to pay indirectly to the government.

Thinking of going on a road trip on your new vehicle? Don't forget toll tax. Thinking of giving a little treat to your friends on the occasion of buying a new vehicle? At least 12% GST in the restaurant.

Pheww! That's heavy and too much to think about, isn't it? You should probably have a drink to let that sink in, but wait!

Say hola to excise duties.

Let us assume that after spending and paying all the bills and taxes, you finally manage to save ₹10,000 and decide to invest it in a Mutual Fund. Any gains arising from such an investment will be taxed as capital gains.

Apart from all these taxes, you also pay municipal taxes, professional taxes, stamp duty and some other import-based taxes.

Many people tend to ignore taxes while planning their wealth. The truth is that, often, in the form of direct and indirect taxes to the state government or the central government, our biggest expenditure is in the form of taxes. To manage our money smartly, the first step is to be aware of what you are paying and how you are paying it.

Being Aware of the Tax Laws

18

Once you figure out the ways in which your cash flows out from your pockets in the form of taxes, you should become aware of the basics of tax laws so that you can have some understanding of what you can do to save taxes. I believe that some basics of taxation should be taught in school itself. You see, taxes are inevitable and the students will have to pay them one day. So, why not make them future-ready? Let's hope this happens some day.

The Income Tax Act prescribes the payment of a self-assessment tax, meaning that the government does not tell you the amount you are required to pay; you have to assess the amount yourself and pay it to the government. If the tax department finds any non-compliance or mismatch, then you are served a notice.

When I say be aware of the taxes that you pay, that does not mean that you handle all your taxes all on your own. I believe it is smart to do it on your own but smarter to hire an expert. You will be able to save more on taxes than the expert's fees you pay.

Before beginning, remember one thing. When we talk about income tax laws, there are many provisions which help you save taxes. The Income Tax Act is not enacted solely to tax all your incomes; it provides several ways to avoid hardships caused by taxation.

Income tax is applicable on all of your 'incomes'. Depending upon your occupation—salaried, businessperson or with passive income—different provisions provide for expenditures or investments that help you save taxes.

Khushi and Tanya paid taxes as well. Both of them bore housing, travel and other expenses, but Khushi was smart and took advantage of all possible deductions such as house rent allowance, leave travel concession, etc., due to which she saved on the overall income tax. When Tanya's salary was ₹1,50,000, her post-tax income used to be almost ₹1,25,000. On the other hand, a couple of years later, when tax rates were unchanged and Khushi's salary was ₹1,50,000, her post-tax income was almost ₹1,32,000. Their tax liabilities were different due to their 'expenditures', which provided Khushi with tax deductions and helped in boosting her Personal Capital.

SELECT A BUSINESS ENTITY WISELY

If you are a business owner, it is important that you select your business entity wisely. A business can run in the form of sole proprietorship, Hindu undivided family (HUF), partnership firm, limited liability partnership firm, private/public companies, trust, etc. The different types of business entities have different structures for taxation. For example, a sole proprietorship form of business has the benefit of slab rates of taxes which are available to individuals but the incidence of surcharge is high. On the other hand, companies and partnership firms are taxed at flat rates.

Thus, if you choose the right business entity, not only will you be able to save taxes, but can manage your compliance burden with ease. Also, whatever form of business you choose, don't forget to keep receipts of your expenditures and consult your advisor if you can claim tax deductions on them or not.

FILE TAX RETURNS REGULARLY

Some people think that filing income tax returns is voluntary and troublesome, thus they tend to avoid doing so.

Filing tax returns is compulsory for everyone earning above a certain threshold, but it is advisable to file tax returns every year even if your tax liability is nil. This will create an income history which will be helpful while applying for loans and credit cards.

If you are a salaried individual, you should be aware if any tax has been deducted from your salary. If TDS is paid, then you can claim it as credit while filing returns and seek refunds of any excess tax deducted.

Also, if you have certain kinds of capital losses, you can adjust it with income of future years, but the condition is that you have to file your tax returns on time.

TAX ADVANTAGE FOR SOME EXPENDITURES

Most people think that only business owners can claim a deduction for every work-related expenditure. This is not completely true. A salaried individual can also claim deduction against some expenditures.

For example, most people know that rent paid can be claimed as a deduction under income tax. You can also claim the deduction of your travelling expenditures under 'leave travel concession'. Try to find out about other deductible expenditures or deductible investments which may be applicable to you.

Some of the most common examples of deductions via investments are contributions to provident fund, pension scheme and ELSS. Some uncommon ones would include investments made to save capital gains.

AVOID BEING TAXED REDUNDANTLY

Once you are aware of the types of taxes you are already paying, you can avoid a lot of double taxation. If you are a business owner registered under GST, don't forget to claim a credit of all the GST paid for any service/goods or capital equipment used for business purposes.

Similarly, if you are paying stamp duty or registration fees while buying a house, it can be claimed as a tax deduction, subject to some limits. Further, if you have paid municipal taxes for a rented-out house property, a deduction can be claimed under the Income Tax Act.

CAR

If you are thinking about buying a car, don't just consider the design, engine and colour. The GST can make a huge difference on your pockets. In India, the taxes on your car vary depending on type (SUV/ sedan/hatchback), engine type (petrol/diesel) and fuel tank capacity. For example, a car with length of 4000 mm (or less) is taxed almost 14% lower than a car with a length of more than 4000 mm. Do you think it's viable to pay thousands of rupees as extra taxes just to add a couple of inches to your vehicle?

My Advice

On the whole, you need to appreciate the fact that tax planning is not something to be organised the day before you file your taxes. It is like a journey that begins the moment you start earning money. You cannot evade taxes altogether; it is a reality of life. But you can plan ahead and save taxes.

At the same time, there is a huge difference between tax planning and tax avoidance. The first is your right. The second is illegal. Do not listen to people who give you wrong advice, no matter who they are. Calculate and pay your taxes honestly and diligently.

Save Money, Not Taxes

19

Paying taxes can be a really painful affair, especially direct taxes, which you have to directly pay the government. We tend to bargain even while buying potatoes, so how can we not try saving taxes? Giving a part of your hard-earned money to the government can be a little overwhelming. Some people go to the extremes trying to save taxes. They tend to make bad choices where they end up losing money instead of saving it.

Some very popular investments that can help you save taxes are contributions to provident funds, and investing in ELSS and National Savings Certificates (NSC). Further, some investments, such as NHAI bonds, are also advised to save capital gain taxes. However, some tax-saving instruments provide very nominal returns.

Let us understand this with an example. Suppose you have an option to save ₹1 lakh in taxes by investing ₹5 lakhs in an instrument providing an annual return of 5% for three years. Do you think it is a wise choice? Let us see.

If you decide to go ahead with the investment, you might save ₹1 lakh in taxes, and would also earn ₹75,000 as interest after three years. So, after three years, you will have ₹5,75,000 with you. Alternatively, if you do not opt for this tax-saving scheme, you would have to pay ₹1 lakh as taxes, but you would be left with ₹4 lakhs to invest at your own discretion. Now, suppose you choose to invest it in a Mutual Fund providing a return of 15% per year. Despite paying income tax of ₹1 lakh, you will be able to make ₹60,000 per year, and your corpus after three years will be ₹5,80,000, so you gained money despite not saving taxes.

But something else can happen, too. If, after paying taxes, you invest your money in a fixed deposit earning 7% interest, your corpus at the end of three years will be ₹4,84,000. So, this is not recommended because you would not have been able to save tax or money. The key is, if you're confident of allocating your funds to better investment instruments, don't go for tax-saving instruments. However, if you doubt your asset allocation skills, tax-saving instruments might be the best option for you.

Always remember, investing in tax-saving instruments depends on how you can invest the rest of the money. Also, generally, tax-saving instruments come with a lock-in period. So your money loses its liquidity and you cannot use it during that time. However, some people may find that having a lock-in period is a great way to stop spending money and keep it invested. Ultimately, the choice is yours. Don't fall into the trap of wasting money just to save tax. Similarly, you cannot opt for a home loan just because it saves taxes. You have to check your financial health and your repayment capability before you decide to go for it.

We should not forget taxation while taking any investment decision. Different instruments are subjected to different rates of taxes. Hence, when you evaluate investment options, it is important that you calculate the post-tax returns. Some investments might provide a return as high as 20% but the gains will be taxed at 30%. This brings your post-tax returns down to 14%.

Take another example. Suppose you choose to invest in a moderately risky instrument providing a return of 10%, where the returns are taxed at 30%.

On the other hand, you had an option of a risk-free instrument providing a tax-free return of 7%, but you decided not to go for it because the returns were lower. If you had calculated, you would have found that your post-tax returns would be the same in both the cases. This means you took all the additional risk just to pay the reward to the government.

So we see that apart from risk, returns and liquidity, taxation is also an important criterion before determining your investment. Let us compare some investment instruments with respect to their post-tax returns.

DEBT FUNDS VS FIXED DEPOSITS

Debt Funds and fixed deposits are the two attractive options available to those who possess funds (money) that are not likely to be consumed in the near future. People may generally go for fixed deposits as they are seen as a safer option. But, it is always better to know about all the options available to you because then you can make an informed decision. So, here's some useful information for you.

While investing in a fixed deposit, you are already aware of the returns that you would be receiving. As of 2020, it is approximately 6%. The tenure of investment can range anywhere between seven days to ten years and the risk is low. Interest receivable from fixed deposits is taxable at the slab rates of the individual. This means, it can be as high as 30%, if you fall into that slab.

If you noticed, I wrote 'interest receivable' and not 'interest received'. This means, if you have invested ₹1 lakh in a fixed deposit for three years, then you might not receive interest in your bank account every year, as it gets reinvested. You will receive the compounded amount of ₹1,19,101 at the end of the third year, but you will be required to pay taxes on a year-to-year basis on the interest accrued.

With regard to Debt Funds, they are also considered as low-risk investments. The fact is, they do come with some risk. A Debt Fund comes with an inherent risk of default. If we talk about returns, they can provide a return of 6–9% depending on the interest rates prevailing in the market. The gains arising from a Debt Fund are taxable only at the time of redemption at the rate of 20% with the benefit of indexation.

If your annual income is taxed between 5% and 20%, then investing in fixed deposits will give you better post-tax returns. In addition, the involved risk will be less and you will have the desired liquidity.

However, if you are being taxed at 30% or higher,

and both FDs and Debt Funds are providing a return of 7%, due to the effect of taxation, the post-tax return on the FD will be 4.9% and for Debt Funds it will be 5.6%. Thus, in order to manage your finances better, before choosing any investment option, don't forget to include taxation in your calculations.

When we talk about Mutual Funds, gains from equity-oriented Mutual Funds are taxed at lower rates than debt-based Mutual Funds. In fact, when we compare each class of asset as an investment option, the taxation differs. So choosing carefully will ultimately make all the difference.

Module:
Insurance

Why Insurance?

20

You might have heard, 'Small things sometimes make a big difference!' So here's how a small insurance amount affected the Personal Capital of Tanya and Khushi.

Both of them purchased an Apple MacBook Air for ₹70,000 each. Apple provides a warranty of one year from the date of purchase with an option to buy a subscription for the Apple Care extended protection plan, or insurance, every year for ₹16,000 per annum. Tanya, being very particular about her cash outflows, chose not to take the insurance and decided to save ₹16,000. She believed it was a smart choice. On the other hand, Khushi realised that for any problem with her MacBook, she would be required to pay at least ₹50,000 for repairs. Now she was a person who focused on her Personal Capital and did not want to risk taking a toll of ₹50,000 on it. So she paid the additional ₹16,000.

When their MacBooks did happen to suffer damage in the second year, Tanya had to pay ₹50,000 for the complete replacement of its motherboard, while Khushi stood protected from this financial loss. This is how insurance helps protect against future uncertainties.

Due to aggressive selling, insurance has earned a somewhat negative reputation. Of course, even I feel irritated when a random call comes from an unknown number saying, 'Good afternoon sir. I'm calling you from xyz insurance company and we have an amazing offer for you.' But just because it is being pushed, does it mean that insurance is unimportant for us? Let's evaluate this in detail.

Insurance is something whose benefits may not be quite visible but its absence has severe disadvantages for sure. While insurance is important, buying the right kind of insurance from the right channel is equally important too. Traditionally, insurance agents sell the products of insurance companies. These agents use the fear factor to sell their products and earn massive commissions. That commission-backed selling did very little good for buyers.

Here are the key concepts about insurance so that you enter into a contract that will actually benefit you and your family.

HOW DOES INSURANCE WORK?

It is always better to start with the basics. So, the basic question is—what exactly is insurance?

An insurance is an agreement between two entities, wherein one promises the other to pay the agreed amount or sum assured in case of any damage or loss of the underwritten asset in return for an insurance premium. These assets could be life, health, automobile, home, electronic gadgets, and so on. It's like an assurance to the policyholders that helps them remain financially safe and secure after an unfortunate event. The duration for which the policyholder is protected is known as the insurance policy period or term.

In today's era, anything and everything can be insured. For instance, David Beckham and Cristiano Ronaldo have their legs insured against all kinds of injuries and disfigurements. Lata Mangeshkar, Amitabh Bachchan and Rajnikant have got their voices insured and Sania Mirza has had her hands insured to keep her financially protected. The learning here is, you have to find the kind of insurance that fulfils your needs.

My suggestion is, you should necessarily get a life and health insurance irrespective of your age, gender or profession. After that, depending upon

your requirements, you can opt to get your devices or your home insured. An insurance will not only offer you some peace of mind but also ensure that your Personal Capital is not affected at the time of crises. You can consider insurance as an investment that will help you at unfortunate times. To get the right insurance, you just have to avoid some mistakes.

Broadly, insurances can be classified into three major categories:

- Life insurance
- Health insurance
- General insurance

The next three chapters will take you through the nuts and bolts of the three insurances categories.

Life Insurance

21

Ever wondered what will happen to your family if something happens to you? That may sound like a life insurance salesperson's pitch, but it's an important question. Almost every family in India depends on a few earning members who bear the burden of every day-to-day activity, including providing for the expenses of the spouse, children and parents. And thus, it is the duty of these earning members to plan for catastrophes. One way to do this is by insuring themselves by purchasing an appropriate life insurance policy after considering factors such as age, expenses, life expectancy, income level, and so on.

As they say, 'Hope for the best but prepare for the worst.' If you don't plan for your success, that's fine. But if you don't plan for your failures, that would be a disaster. What I mean is, if you are able to create sufficient Personal Capital for yourself, good. But if you're not, you should have some back-up.

If you don't have sufficient insurance cover yet, it is important to get it quickly. Unforeseen tragedies like illness or injury or death can cause substantial emotional trauma for your family and loved ones. A financial stress on top of that will be very difficult to manage. Death is inevitable, but it helps to prepare for it.

Purchasing insurance is a method of financial planning where individuals can insure themselves or their assets against future uncertainties. Life insurance is simply insurance of life where the insurer (the company that provides the insurance coverage) promises to pay a predefined sum of money to the designated beneficiary if the policyholder expires during the term of the policy. The policyholder is required to pay the agreed premium for this.

Insurance policies can be customised based on the policyholder's requirements to provide more flexibility. This flexibility comes in the form of added services that you can opt for after paying an additional premium. These additional services are called 'riders'. Riders can be of the following types:

ACCIDENTAL DEATH RIDER

Generally, life insurance covers death by natural causes or accident, but this rider provides an additional sum to the beneficiary in case the insured person dies because of an accident.

CRITICAL ILLNESS RIDER

With the addition of this rider to your insurance policy, you are entitled to receive a particular amount if you are diagnosed with any of the critical illnesses listed in the policy document. The illnesses may vary across insurance companies, but usually include ailments like cancer, heart attack, brain tumour and any major organ transplant.

DISABILITY RIDER

If you become disabled temporarily or permanently in an accident, then this rider entitles you to receive a periodic payment for some time (five or ten years). Thus you have some income when you are unable to work.

INCOME BENEFIT RIDER

This rider ensures regular or uniform income to the beneficiary for a specified period in case of the demise of an insured person. This rider is recommended for individuals who are the sole earning members of the family.

WAIVER OF PREMIUM RIDER

If you are unable to pay premiums because of a disability or an unfortunate event, then all the future premiums are waived off by the insurer. The inability to pay a premium does not affect the benefits specified in the policy.

I believe that one should definitely opt for the accidental death rider and critical illness rider. The rest depends on your profile and how you assess the risks.

WHO SHOULD TAKE INSURANCE?

To secure and maintain the financial stability of the family, the breadwinner must buy an insurance policy. These breadwinners may include:

Parents

Parents are the source of finance in any family. Every parent wants a good future for their children, but what will happen to such dreams if the earning parent passes away or has a serious illness or an accident? Who will take care of their children's educational expenses? So parents must buy insurance to secure their and their children's future.

Young Professionals

Many young professionals are not married and do not have any family responsibilities. But they may get married soon and have to support their families. Even if they do not have any plans to get married immediately, the uncertainties linked with life, such as illnesses or accidents, cannot be ignored. So they should purchase insurance. It is good to buy insurance when you are young because the premium is low and it will remain the same until the end of the policy.

Newly Married Couples

Generally, newly married couples exchange a lot of gifts, but the first gift they should give each other should be a life insurance policy. It is a long-lasting gift that will take care of the financial needs of the spouse after the insured person passes away.

Working Women

Women in today's world are not just equal to men but far ahead of them in many areas. Many families are dependent on the earnings of women, which makes it the responsibility of such breadwinners to secure their loved ones financially.

Self-Employed People

There is higher variability in the earnings of a self-employed person as compared to a salaried person. Often, such individuals take a personal or a business loan, which makes it more critical to secure their families from unforeseen circumstances. If you are a self-employed person, then you should always have an insurance policy.

Retirees

Generally, retirees do not have to take care of the expenses of their children, but to secure their spouse's and their own future, they need to purchase an appropriate insurance policy.

Credit Takers

People take all kinds of loans—personal loans, home loans, education loans, and so on. Many unemployed and self-employed people have to take credit for a short or a long term. If something happens to you, all the responsibility of repayment will fall on your family. So if you have taken a loan, you need to buy insurance.

Life insurance carries double benefits for taxpayers—the premium paid is allowed as a deduction from taxable income under section 80C, and the maturity value is also exempt from tax subject to certain conditions.

HOW MUCH INSURANCE DO YOU NEED?

Life insurance ensures that the insured person's family receives the payment after his or her death. Under-insurance can result in a severe financial crisis. You should be extremely careful about the 'sum assured'. Don't forget to account for the following factors before making a decision:

Number of Dependents and Their Expenses

Dependents can be spouses, children and parents whose financial needs have to be taken care of. These may be expenses for education, marriage or an illness, in addition to their day-to-day expenses.

Loan Obligations

To fulfil your dreams, you might have taken a loan for a home or a car or might have started investments which need regular premiums to be paid. Such expenses should be considered while calculating the sum assured.

Lifestyle

What kind of lifestyle do you want to provide for your family? If they have to stay in an expensive city or locality, you need to adjust the sum assured accordingly.

Other Financial Obligations

You need to carefully consider any other financial obligations such as debt, rent or other expenses that might be there.

Ideally, your life insurance should be at least ten times your current annual income. This will ensure that your family has sufficient funds to meet their routine requirements and maintain the current standard of life. If you have a huge debt or a higher number of dependents, you should increase the amount. There are many online tools where you can calculate the sum assured required based on your current age, expenses, current net worth, expected inflation rate, life expectancy, financial goals, and so on.

Now let us look at the different kinds of life insurance plans offered by companies and how you can select the right plan.

TERM INSURANCE POLICY

It is the type of life insurance that provides financial protection to the nominee in case the policyholder dies during the term of the insurance. The policy has a limited coverage period and is one of the most cost-effective life insurance schemes, with the lowest premium. This kind of a policy is also suitable when you have taken a loan. For example, if you take a twenty-year home loan, you should take a corresponding twenty-year term insurance. In case of your death, your family will have enough funds to pay off the loan without a problem.

I have seen people not opting for term insurance because the insurer provides no return if the policyholder survives the term of the policy. Let's first look at other types of life insurance policies before we discuss this.

ENDOWMENT POLICY

An endowment policy is a life insurance policy with a maturity benefit after the insurance term. If the insured person dies during the term of the policy, the beneficiary receives the sum assured. If the insured person survives the term of the insurance, then they are entitled to receive a maturity benefit. In effect, it gives a return of 1–6% to the policyholder on maturity.

This feature makes it a popular product among Indian customers since the plan provides triple benefits— death benefit, maturity benefit and tax savings.

These policies are of two types: 'with-profit' and 'without-profit'. If an insurance company earns a profit, then that profit will be distributed among with-profit endowment policyholders. But such insured persons have to pay an extra premium to opt for the with-profit feature. In the without-profit policy, profits are not shared with policyholders, but the premium is relatively less.

Endowment policies come with a feature of surrender value. The policyholder can discontinue the plan after a certain period, and receive an amount called the 'surrender value'.

Why do people prefer an endowment plan?

Psychologically, they want to receive something back if they survive the term period. They don't want to 'lose' the premiums paid. People think it has the benefits of both insurance as well as an investment, as they will get 'assured' returns.

What are the negatives of endowment plans?

Endowment plans provide a lower sum assured as compared to term plans. Also, the return on the investment is very low, much lower than inflation rate, so the value of your investment diminishes.

UNIT LINKED INSURANCE PLAN

The Unit Linked Insurance Plan, or ULIP, is an endowment plan with a slight difference in the returns on investment. It is presented as a combination of insurance and investment. The investment part of the premium is placed in capital market instruments as specified by the policyholder, who bears the entire risk of market fluctuations. These investment instruments can be equity, debt, money markets and the like.

Generally, insurance is bought for a prolonged period. It is also said that you need to stay invested for a prolonged period to get better returns from the capital markets. Therefore, insurance agents sell ULIPs as an investment that provides a source of good returns along with life cover. Unlike other traditional plans, ULIPs come with several customisations which might provide a great deal of choice and flexibility.

WHOLE LIFE INSURANCE POLICY

A whole life insurance policy is similar to an endowment plan that provides death benefits to the beneficiary and has an additional component of savings attached to it. It is called a whole-life plan because it provides cover for the insured person for the duration of their life as long as premiums are paid on time. The maturity age for this policy is 100 years—if the insured person survives the age of 100 years, then the policy becomes an endowment policy and the policyholder gets the maturity benefit.

MONEY BACK POLICY

Money back policy is similar to endowment plans but with a small difference. A fixed proportion of the sum assured is paid out at specified intervals during the duration of the policy. In case of the demise of the insured person, the beneficiary receives the full sum assured along with profits or bonuses, if opted for.

My Opinion

As mentioned earlier, I have seen people not opting for term insurance because the insurer provides no return if the policyholder survives the term of the policy. But of all the different types of life insurances available, I suggest opting for a term insurance. With term insurance, you risk neither being underinsured nor creating an imbalance in your regular budget by paying huge insurance premiums. I feel endowment plans are just a way through which insurance companies take advantage of our fears. They say an endowment plan provides a guaranteed return, but at what cost? Look at the following example:

If I am twenty-six years old, need insurance for twenty-one years and am willing to deposit ₹10,000 every month, then as per a typical endowment plan, my sum assured will be ₹25,65,000.

This means, if anything happens to me, my family will receive ₹25,65,000 (the sum assured) along with a bonus, if applicable. And at the end of the term of the policy, I will receive around ₹54,00,000 (the maturity amount). My payments or investment in this case will be 10,000 x 12 x 21 = ₹25,20,000. This is a return of around 3.5%, even lower than a savings bank account.

Instead, if I opt for a term plan, the premium per month is less than ₹1,000, while if anything happens to me, my family will receive ₹1 crore. But if you buy an endowment plan for your family to receive ₹1 crore (the sum assured), you have to pay around ₹23,000 a month if you are twenty-six years old.

Just by choosing the right plan, you can not only provide your family a better future but also save ₹22,000 per month. Now, if you invest this ₹22,000 every month in a Mutual Fund earning 10% for twenty-one years, you receive ₹1.89 crores. This will ensure that your family is never under-insured and also provides you with an excellent corpus on retirement.

People generally prefer endowment plans over term plans because the endowment plan ensures you get your money back along with interest after the term of the policy. In contrast, in a term plan, you get nothing if you survive the policy term. But if we go through the numbers, the endowment plan offers not only a very low interest rate but also insufficient protection to your family. In contrast, term plans are cheaper. Even if they don't return your money, you can still save the premium you would have paid otherwise and invest it to get a higher return. This ensures utmost protection of your family as well as wealth creation.

We have to realise that we pay virtually nothing for term plans while we get virtually nothing in endowment plans.

TERM PLAN: IMPORTANT FACTORS

To identify and purchase an apt term plan for yourself, the following points should be considered and implemented:

Coverage

Buy a term insurance plan with significant coverage and only up to retirement age. We all have financial responsibilities when we are young, and they keep increasing with age. But at the same time, our assets or investments are also growing and moving towards maturity. Eventually, the dependents will start earning and become independent. Therefore, it makes sense to buy term insurance with a large sum assured when you are young, and its tenure should be not more than your retirement age.

Terms and Conditions

Do not get attracted to lucrative-sounding offers which promise huge returns. There are a lot of offerings in the market promising various benefits such as '₹1 crore term plan at just ₹30 per day'. Such offers come with hidden conditions and are just a way of selling the policy. Check the terms and conditions in detail and take advice from professionals before signing up.

Riders or Add-Ons

With the addition of every rider, the benefits of the term plan increase. Riders add value to your policy, but it is essential to choose the appropriate ones.

Every rider increases your premium, which must be paid throughout the policy. It's your hard-earned money, and even a small portion of it should be invested wisely.

The risk of being in an accident increases if you are a frequent traveller. So in that case, you can add an accidental death rider. If your family has a history of heart attack or other critical illness, then you can add a critical illness rider.

Declare All Information

The main reason for claims being rejected is not providing important information in the beginning. Many people do not mention being a smoker or that they drink alcohol so that they can pay a lower premium for the policy. Also, people hide critical health information to reduce premiums. This is wrong in the eyes of the law. Hiding facts is a breach of contract with the insurer and will result in your claim being rejected. You will end up losing all the premiums you have paid and not get any benefit of the policy.

Read Policy Documents Carefully

It is imperative to check and verify the policy documents after purchasing a policy. These documents contain all your information such as name, date of birth, blood group, nominee details, medical information and other essential facts about you. If there are any errors, then get them rectified immediately because any discrepancy may result in your claim being rejected. Also, check that all the benefits and other conditions that you are expecting have been clearly mentioned in the policy documents. These documents are the only thing that will be relied on while settling the claims and disputes between you and the insurance company. All these checks and verifications are essential as they are the reason behind opting for a particular policy. Insurance companies also provide a 'free look' period which offers an option to opt-out if you have made a mistake or changed your mind. This means, even after buying a policy you will have an option to opt out.

A Reliable Brand

Companies provide a host of services based on which their brand value is determined. These services define the experience that a customer gets and how satisfied he or she is. This includes the overall purchase and claim settlement experience. Claim settlement ratio and settlement time are essential features to be considered to check the real performance of the insurance company. These are the primary reasons why you purchased the insurance in the first place. Don't forget to check the number of complaints associated with the policy and insurance company. All this information is available online.

Communicate with Your Family

You buy an insurance policy to protect the financial condition of your loved ones. So they need to know about such investments. At times, it may be difficult or awkward for you to have such conversations with your family members, but it is the right thing to do, and it should be done immediately after purchasing any insurance policy.

Beware of Over-Insurance

At the time of taking an insurance policy, you will be asked to declare your existing policies. This is because insurance policies decide the coverage based on Human Life Value (HLV). So if you do not declare your existing policies correctly, you will end up paying excess premium without any benefits. In fact, non-disclosures might end up creating complications at the time of claim settlement.

Health Insurance

22

Will you remain completely healthy and fit for the next few years? Looking at the lifestyle that most people have nowadays, there's no guarantee of this. The cost of medical treatment is increasing due to rising inflation, new cures and new technology. These high costs and limited government support make it difficult for citizens to live a financially healthy life, especially for the middle and lower classes of the country. In such a situation, absence of health insurance will affect your Personal Capital adversely.

Hospitalisation can empty your pockets much sooner than you realise. Imagine a situation in which the sole breadwinner or any family member is hospitalised. How will the funds for the treatment be arranged? This is where health insurance enters the picture.

Health insurance is a type of insurance that provides financial assistance in case of medical emergencies.

The insurance company will take care of your medical expenses and you are expected to pay regular premiums for an agreed period of time. A good health insurance policy would cover pre-hospitalisation, hospitalisation and post-hospitalisation expenses. This includes expenses for medical check-ups, transportation, consultation, treatment and medicines.

HOW MUCH HEALTH INSURANCE DO YOU NEED?

Although there is no ideal method to calculate this amount, there are two broadly accepted thumb rules to help you calculate the minimum sum required.

The first rule says you should have a health cover of at least 50% of your annual income plus 100% of the consolidated medical expenses for the last three years. The second rule says you should have a cover which is sufficient for a coronary artery bypass surgery in a hospital of your choice.

Ideally, you should opt for a health cover of minimum ₹5 lakhs. There are family floater plans which allow you to include your family members as well. In a family floater plan, it is advised to opt for a policy that provides health cover of ₹20 lakhs for a family of two adults and two kids.

At the same time, it is imperative to determine your premium-paying capacity. If you fail to pay a premium on time, it may cost you some penalty or you may lose the entire benefits of the policy. A figure of 2% of your annual income can be used as an indicator of your premium-paying capacity. Now, you can review this along with the health cover calculated previously.

Suppose you concluded that the required sum assured should be ₹20 lakhs for your family, which can be bought at a premium of ₹20,000 per year. On the other hand, your annual income is just ₹8 lakhs, which makes your premium-paying capacity only ₹16,000 per year. For the time being, you can reduce your sum assured requirement (to, say, ₹15 lakhs), and buy a health cover accordingly. As your income goes up, you can increase the insurance amount.

CHECKLIST FOR A HEALTH INSURANCE POLICY

Health insurance is a complex form of insurance. Avoid buying health insurance through agents. They are not necessarily your well-wishers and may not guide you towards a policy most suited to you. Follow this checklist before purchasing a policy:

Calculate the Sum Assured Required

It is essential to calculate the sum assured because any expenses above that amount will not be covered under a health insurance policy. So you should carefully understand your needs and requirements.

Claim Settlement Efficiency

Claim settlement ratio and settlement time are crucial parameters to be considered to check the actual performance, reliability and trustworthiness of the company.

Sub-Limits

Health insurance comes with many terms and conditions. Sub-limits are conditions that put limits on your benefits. Insurance companies put caps on expenses such as room rates per day, ambulance charges and ICU charges. You are allowed to claim only a certain percentage of the health cover on such expenses. In some cases, the limits, say on room rates, may make the entire policy worthless for you. So read the clause of sub-limits very carefully.

Riders and Top-Ups

We already know that it is difficult to calculate the right sum assured. The rising costs of treatment make it even more difficult to arrive at a specific number. But you can analyse your health condition and accordingly choose riders or top-ups which can provide additional benefits with a nominal increase in premium. At the same time, you should not opt for all available riders and top-ups, as this may result in additional expense with not much value addition.

Pre- and Post-Hospitalisation Coverage

Medical expenses occur not only on hospitalisation but also before hospitalisation and often post-hospitalisation as well. Before hospitalisation, you will need to go through a series of consultations, diagnostic tests and medications that should be covered by your health insurance policy. Similarly, you usually incur additional expenses post-hospitalisation because of follow-up visits for consultations, tests and medicines. Therefore, check the terms and conditions for pre- and post-hospitalisation benefits.

Day-Care Coverage

To avail the benefits of a health insurance policy, you are usually required to be admitted for at least twenty-four hours in a hospital. But many procedures such as cataract surgeries and fracture treatments do not require an overnight stay in a hospital. Your health insurance company should ideally cover such expenses. But this will come at an additional cost in terms of a higher premium. So evaluate the cost-benefit carefully.

Network Hospitals

Insurance companies collaborate with hospitals, clinics and medical professionals. The insurance companies get lower rates from them and, in return, send patients through their customer network. The facility of cashless mediclaim can only be availed at such hospitals. The insurance company will settle your bills with the hospitals directly. You only have to pay the excess amount, which is not covered by the policy, to the hospital, clinic or medical professional. On the other hand, if you get treatment in a non-network hospital, then you have to pay the entire bill first and then claim reimbursement later. This can take time and there is always a chance of making an error in the paperwork. Therefore, before purchasing a policy, check the list of network hospitals and ensure that there is a hospital nearby where you can go comfortably and with confidence.

Waiting Period

It is mandatory to disclose one's entire medical history at the time of applying for a policy. All health insurance plans cover pre-existing ailments only after a certain period, often after three or four years. This period may vary with the type of illness. Check that you find this waiting period manageable.

Co-Payment Clause

Many policies come with a clause of co-payment, where the policyholder pays some amount of the bill. A co-payment clause usually reduces the premium amount. Some policies may have a co-payment clause for some procedures only.

No-Claim Bonus

Some policies, but not all, come with the benefit of a no-claim bonus, that is, you will get a benefit if you do not make any claim during the year. The insurance company may give you some discount on premium or they may increase the sum assured. So read policy documents carefully.

Exclusions

There are many illnesses whose treatment and tests are not covered in health insurance policies. Also, according to the Insurance Regulatory and Development Authority of India (IRDAI), the insurance company can reject the claim if a policyholder violates the rules related to exclusions. It is recommended to read the exclusions section carefully to ensure you get a suitable policy.

Online Platforms

There are several online platforms that provide a host of insurance services. You can also get basic information on insurance products and compare the different policies available. All these services are without any cost. But most will seek your email address and your mobile number so that they can send you offers later.

These platforms can provide complete guidance and assistance in purchasing policies based on your specifications. At the same time, it is also possible that they may suggest expensive policies just to provide multiple benefits. So use these platforms with care. If you do not trust them, you can consult your financial advisor and book a policy, but that might come at a slightly extra cost.

Health insurance offers some tax benefits to the policyholder. These tax benefits are provided to encourage people to take health insurance. My advice is, don't procrastinate. Get health insurance now!

General Insurance

23

Genera insurance is the insurance for all types of assets that you possess, except life. Hence, it is also called non-life insurance. This is an agreement between the policyholder and the insurer to protect the assets for a specified period in exchange for a periodic premium. Buying general insurance is like buying peace of mind as it makes you relaxed and saves you from additional financial burden in case of loss, damage or theft of your valuables.

These are the common types of general insurance available:

- Motor insurance
- Home insurance
- Travel insurance
- Fire insurance
- Crop insurance
- Marine insurance
- Commercial insurance

You can opt for general insurance for your business or to secure an expensive asset. What's important is that you go through the insurance documents carefully, be aware of the coverage, and don't forget to compare the different policies available.

In the end, I would just like to say that insurance is a protection for you like an anchor in times of financial thunderstorms. While you are busy creating Personal Capital for yourself, insurance will provide you support during unforeseen events, just like an emergency fund.

Module:
Mis-Selling

Financial Mis-Selling

24

Have you ever seen a doctor administering polio drops to a sixty-year-old person? That would be totally absurd, right? We know that polio drops are useless for an adult. But, just for a moment, suppose a doctor has been promised a fully-paid trip abroad, along with his or her family, if they successfully administer polio drops to a hundred people in a week. Do you think all doctors will consider the patient's age? Most will, but some may not.

Sometimes sales agents, to meet their high targets or earn extra commissions, might try to sell you financial services that you may not require at all. Careful planning and a keen awareness can help you stay one step ahead of the game.

WHAT IS FINANCIAL MIS-SELLING?

Financial mis-selling is when a person is convinced to purchase a product or service that does not satisfy their needs. It may involve misrepresenting the attributes of the product or service or suggesting an inappropriate option to a customer even though it clearly does not suit their needs.

There can be two types of mis-selling:

- Material Mis-selling: This is when the seller provides the customer with incorrect, incomplete or false information. The salesperson tries to depict a product as something that it is clearly not.

- Suitability Mis-selling: This is when the salesperson tries to sell a product or service to a customer that may not be suitable for them by omitting or hiding some of the riskier features of the product or service.

Let us look at some instances of mis-selling:

Direct vs Regular Mutual Fund Plans

As I mentioned earlier, Mutual Funds can be of two types: direct or regular. These two Mutual Fund plans are essentially the same and invest in the same instruments. The only difference is the amount of commission charged and hence the returns to the investors. The direct plan requires no payment of commission, so the returns are higher, while the regular plan requires the payment of commission to the distributor and the agent. Before investing in any Mutual Fund, ensure that you are choosing a direct plan over regular ones.

Bank Lockers

In banks, usually you are told, 'There are no lockers available right now.' This is because the demand for lockers is more than their supply. So banks leverage this for their benefit. They try to tie up the facility of a locker with another service. For example, they may say that the limited number of lockers would be available only to premium customers who are willing to purchase a ULIP or an FD from them. This is mis-selling as the investors are forced to invest in avenues they do not want.

ULIPs and Endowment Policies

When a customer wants to purchase a term insurance to cover their risks, often the agent will advise them to purchase a ULIP plan, claiming it provides better returns. However, the problem with ULIPs is that the risk cover they offer is low and the premiums are high. Similar is the case with endowment plans.

Fixed Deposit vs Balanced Funds

An investor may want to invest in a fixed deposit but the agent may push for a Balanced Fund. They would tempt the investor with the higher returns which a Balanced Fund would supposedly provide. Now, though the returns may be higher, the risk involved in Balanced Funds is also higher, and this may not be suitable for the investor. It is not just that there is no guarantee of return to the investor, there may actually be negative returns on some occasions.

HOW CAN YOU SAFEGUARD YOURSELF FROM SUCH FINANCIAL MIS-SELLING?

Financial mis-selling is something that has been going on for a long time and is unlikely to stop, so here's my list of recommendations to enable you to make the best choices for yourself.

Have Full Knowledge

Be aware of the product's features before deciding to purchase it. In order to understand the product better, you can also refer to a checklist:

- Does the product offer fixed returns or returns that are linked to the market? The latter involves more risk and so may not be suitable for all.
- The agent might try to push an unsuitable product by using complicated jargon and confusing you. If you don't understand a product, don't buy it.

- Read all the documents carefully and make sure there are no hidden charges or conditions involved.

- Before purchasing a product, you should also check whether the product is verified and approved by the regulator or government authority.

- The returns that are forecasted are often exaggerated by the distributors and seem very attractive. Often they have not taken taxes into account. After paying taxes, the returns may not look that great after all.

- Also check for the lock-in period involved. Lock-in periods affect the liquidity of the product and may not be viable for some customers.

- Watch out for hybrid or mixed products. Evaluating them can be confusing. These products are easier to fall prey to.

Agent vs Advisor

Investors should be careful as to whose opinions they are seeking. Agents have the incentive of commissions and have to chase targets. Hence, they might try to push their products and services to the customers, even if they are not the ideal solutions. Their commissions are included in the purchase price or investment returns, so they are not obvious. Agents might present themselves to be your well-wisher, but may actually prevent you from taking a wise decision.

On the other hand, advisors may charge an upfront fee, but they are likely to suggest solutions keeping the client's welfare in mind. They also take into account the customer's ability and willingness to take risks.

Know Your Rights

We as customers should also be aware of the different rights that we have if we get duped by banks or insurance companies. If there is a problem, the customer must first raise a complaint with their bank or respective insurance or Mutual Fund company. If no response is received in thirty days, then the customer can escalate the complaint. For banks, the customer can contact the banking ombudsman. They can even file an online complaint on RBI's website or go to the Consumer Forum. If there is any fraud by investment advisors or portfolio managers, they can file a complaint on SEBI's SCORE portal.

In Conclusion

The creation of Personal Capital takes time, patience and consistency. You just need to make a few choices correctly and let time perform its magic. Whether you believe it or not, time is really powerful! It possesses the power to transform your piggy bank into a money-making machine. If you're still asking 'How', go back to the chapters in order to understand.

The sole purpose of writing this book is to guide you through your journey of personal finance. Having read this book, you should be able to manage your personal finances in such a way that your future is the same as Khushi's. You can do it and you should do it! I would love to watch you 'Mint Your Money'!

Acknowledgements

We humans prefer to take centre stage and tend to feel important as a part of this universe. We're usually happy residing in our fantasy world, in which anything and everything revolves around us. But that is where a small 'Dhanyawaad', i.e. 'Thank You', makes us realise the importance of everything that is not 'us'. It makes us realise that we are not just what we are because of ourselves, but all the people, situations, circumstances and opportunities that have contributed to constitute our present.

Someone rightly said, 'Gratitude makes sense of our past, brings peace for today and creates a vision for tomorrow.' I already believed in this, but writing Mint Your Money strengthened my belief in the maxim. I'm grateful to everyone who contributed to the creation, compilation, editing and publishing of this personal finance guide, which I hope accurately represents the Indian perspective.

I would like to begin by thanking CA Panjul Agrawal for helping me make this book a reality. It would have never seen the light of the day if she hadn't agreed to help me. She has been a brilliant colleague, friend and the most competent mind at my disposal to bounce off ideas and refine concepts. I will be forever grateful for her efforts and the honest intent with which she made sure that nothing missed my scrutiny.

Secondly, I am indebted to Ratan Deep Singh for his Midas touch in making sure that the intended message has been delivered in an entertaining yet educative manner. This book would be of much less intellectual value without his copywriting skills! He has helped with his creative instincts and 'Grammar Nazism'. Although he claims to not understand finance, he was able to contribute so much to this book.

The eye-catching images that you see in this book have been designed by our extremely talented graphic designer Mohit Malviya.

A special vote of thanks goes to Deepthi Talwar

and Westland Publications. Without them, this book would not have been conceptualised, and you wouldn't have been able to read it.

I also want to thank God, my parents and my good friends from the bottom of my heart. They indirectly contributed a lot in making this book possible. Having conversations with my parents and friends really helped refine the contents of this book and incorporate a real-life perspective.

Talking about indirect contributions, most of the employees of Finology Ventures Pvt. Ltd have tried their best to contribute in any way they could. I can't thank them all enough.

I may not have been able to include on this page the names of all the people who helped me, but I genuinely feel thankful towards all those who contributed towards making this book happen.

Finally, thank you, reader, for purchasing and reading this. I hope you enjoy reading the book, and I hope you are able to Mint Your Money!